# Chinese Civil Procedure and the Conflict of Laws

CHEN Wei-zuo

Homa & Sekey Books
Tsinghua University Press

FIRST EDITION



---

Library of Congress Cataloging-in-Publication Data

Chen, Weizuo.
Chinese civil procedure and the conflict of laws / Chen Weizuo. -- 1st ed.
p. cm.
Includes index.
ISBN 978-1-931907-83-5 (hardcover)
1. Civil procedure--China. 2. Conflict of law--China. I. Title.
KNQ1710.C44 2012
347.51'05--dc23
2012012913

---

Published by Homa & Sekey Books
3rd Floor, North Tower
Mack-Cali Center III
140 E. Ridgewood Ave.
Paramus, NJ 07652

Tel: 201-261-8810; 800-870-HOMA
Fax: 201-261-8890; 201-384-6055
Email: info@homabooks.com
Website: www.homabooks.com

Printed in U.S.A.
1 3 5 7 9 10 8 6 4 2

# About the Author

CHEN Weizuo, Director of the Research Centre for Private International Law and Comparative Law, Tsinghua University School of Law. Doctor of Laws, Wuhan University, China; LL.M. and *doctor iuris*, *Universität des Saarlandes*, Germany; associate professor at Tsinghua University School of Law, Beijing, China (since 2004); *professeur invité à la Faculté internationale de droit comparé de Strasbourg*, France (since 2003); *professeur invité à l'Université de Strasbourg*, France (2005-2010); to teach a special course in French, *La nouvelle codification du droit international privé chinois*, from 30 July to 3 August 2012 at the Hague Academy of International Law during its 2012 summer session of private international law. Address: Tsinghua University School of Law, 100084 Beijing, China. E-mail: chenwz@mail.tsinghua.edu.cn.

Publications include 6 monographs, 32 articles in Chinese, English, French and German, 14 translations of articles and foreign or international legal documents as well as 4 contributions to works. In particular: CHEN Weizuo, *Latin-Chinese Dictionary of Legal Terms and Maxims*, Law Press China, Beijing, 2009 ; *Comparative Private International Law*, in Chinese, Tsinghua University Press, Beijing, 2008 ; *The General Part of the German Civil Code*, in Chinese, Law Press China, Beijing, 2007; *German Civil Code* (BGB, translated and annotated), Law Press China, Beijing, 2004 (First Edition), 2006 (Second Edition), 2010 (Third Edition); *Rück- und Weiterverweisung (Renvoi) in staatsvertraglichen Kollisionsnormen* (doctoral thesis in German), Peter Lang *Europäischer Verlag der Wissen-*

*schaften*, Frankfurt am Main, 2004 (http://www.hcch.net/ index_en.php?act=text.display&tid=82); *A Study of the Swiss Code on Private International Law* (doctoral thesis in Chinese), Law Press China, Beijing, 1998.

# Preface

The manuscript of the present textbook has been used for a course taught by the author for the LL.M. Program in Chinese Law at Tsinghua University School of Law from 2005 to 2010. The main objective of this course is to provide international students with basic knowledge of Chinese civil procedure and the conflict of laws. In particular, the course expounds civil lawsuits that are filed in accordance with the Chinese code of civil procedure (Civil Procedure Law of the People's Republic of China), other statutes and judicial interpretations, as well as choice of law rules determining the law applicable to civil relationships involving foreign elements. The course provides succinct explanations of essential issues, fundamental principles and particular institutions in Chinese civil procedure and the conflict of laws.

The textbook begins with a survey of the Chinese procedural law and an overview of Chinese civil procedure and then focuses on essential aspects of court jurisdiction and trial procedure in civil matters. In view of the traditional importance of alternative dispute resolution in China, mediation (conciliation) and arbitration are also discussed with corresponding comparisons to civil procedure.

The textbook also discusses issues relating to the conflict of laws, *i.e.* international jurisdiction under the Chinese international civil procedure law, recognition and enforcement of foreign judgments as well as Chinese choice of law rules. Focus is directed toward the Chinese Statute on the Application of Laws to Civil Relationships Involving Foreign

Elements of 28 October 2010, which entered into force on 1 April 2011.

The author owes great thanks to Kevin M. Moore (LL.M., Peking University; Legislative Aide, Oregon Senator Floyd Prozanski; *juris doctor* candidate, Willamette University College of Law) and Thomas Carsten Bork (*stud. iur.*, *Westfälische Wilhelms-Universität Münster*, LL.M. candidate at Tsinghua University School of Law, Beijing) for their great support and many helpful suggestions.

CHEN Weizuo
Beijing
June 8, 2011

# CONTENTS

## Part I Chinese Civil Procedure



## Part II The Conflict of Laws

# Part I Chinese Civil Procedure

# Chapter One A General Survey of Chinese Procedural Law

## I. Substantive and Procedural Law

The legal system of the People's Republic of China (hereinafter referred to as "PRC") – like legal systems both of the Continental civil law family and the Anglo-American law family – knows the classification of substantive law and procedural law. Substantive law deals with rights and obligations that each legal subject (natural person, legal person or any other organization) enjoys and undertakes, whereas procedural law deals with the enforcement of those substantive rights and obligations. In case of a dispute, procedural law functions as a mechanism to realise and enforce the rights stipulated by substantive law. It is said that "substantive law is concerned with what, whereas procedural law is concerned with how".[1]

The relationship between substantive and procedural law is that between essence and form. Without substantive law, procedural law is of no purpose; without procedural law, substantive law cannot be enforced.

The impact of procedural law is enormous in a country like China, which traditionally lacked a culture of rule of law. In traditional Chinese law, not only were civil law and criminal law indistinctly classified, but substantive law and proce-

1 Zhu Yikun, *China's Procedural Law*, Law Press China, Beijing 2003, p. 1.

dural law were not distinguished from one another. As a matter of fact, there was no real procedural law in traditional Chinese law. In recent years, procedural fairness has become a meaningful topic which is beneficial to the construction of rule of law in China.

## II. Different Types of Procedural Law

### A. Civil Procedural Law

The code of civil procedure *i.e.* the Civil Procedure Law (hereinafter referred to as "CPL") of the PRC was adopted at the 4th Session of the Seventh National People's Congress (hereinafter referred to as "NPC") on 9 April 1991, amended in accordance with the Decision on Amending the CPL of the PRC adopted at the 30th Session of the Standing Committee of the Tenth NPC on 28 October 2007. The amendments came into effect on 1 April 2008.

### B. Criminal Procedural Law

For criminal procedural law, there is a criminal procedural code *i.e.* the Criminal Procedure Law of the PRC, which was adopted by the NPC on 1 July 1979. It was one of the first major statutes enacted as part of the nation's effort at rebuilding the legal system at the early stage of reform and opening to the outside world.[2] The criminal procedure code has been revised extensively by the NPC on 17 March 1996. The revised version became effective on 1 January 1997.

---

2 See Daniel C.K. Chow, The Legal System of the People's Republic of China in a Nutshell, Thomson West 2003, pp. 257-258.

## C. Administrative Procedural Law

For the procedures governing administrative litigation, there is the Administrative Litigation Law of 4 April 1989, which entered into effect on 1 October 1990. It provides the basic statutory rules on procedural matters in the area of administrative law. In traditional Chinese law, there has been a concept stating that ordinary citizens could not challenge the legality of concrete administrative acts undertaken by the government. The Administrative Litigation Law was the first Chinese statute of public law character to expressly recognize the right to challenge governmental authority and to allow ordinary citizens, legal persons and other organizations to challenge the legality of concrete administrative acts of governments at various levels.

Besides, the Administrative Review Regulation of 1990, the State Compensation Law of 1994 and the Administrative Penalties Law of 1996 also belong to the major enactments in administrative procedural law.

## D. Statutes and Regulations on Alternative Dispute Resolution

In addition to the statutes on litigation procedures, there are also statutes and regulations regarding alternative dispute resolution (ADR), which are based on non-litigation settlement of disputes by means like mediation and arbitration.

Provisions regarding mediation are contained, for example, in the Organic Rules for People's Mediation Committees of 1989 and in the Measures for Handling Disputes among the People of 1990.

As to arbitration, the Law on Arbitration of 31 March

1994 was adopted by the Standing Committee of the NPC (thus non-basic law), entered into effect on 1 September 1995. Jurisdiction of arbitration institutions has been substantially enlarged under the Law on Arbitration. Arbitration commissions are set up under government organs with higher qualifications for arbitrators. A challenge system is provided in order to ensure the impartiality of arbitrators.

## III. Judicial System of the PRC

### A. Judicial Power and Judicial Organs

In the PRC, the judicial power of the State originates in the legislature, *i.e.* the people's congresses at national and local levels as well as their standing committees.

In the PRC, people's courts, people's procuratorates, public security organs, judicial administrative organs, and State security organs are considered the judicial organs. The function of public security organs is to maintain social and public order, and to conduct investigation and the arrest of criminal suspects. The functions of the judicial administrative organs include the administration of prisons, implementing the system of reform and re-education through labor, and the administration of lawyers and notaries. The functions of State security organs include investigating cases of espionage and special agents. They may also exercise powers of investigation, detention, preliminary examination, and arrest.

### B. People's Courts

#### 1. General Principles

In the PRC, the State adjudicative power is exercised by

the people's courts.[3] Article 123 of the Constitution of the PRC of 1982 (hereinafter referred to as "Constitution") provides that the people's courts in the PRC are the adjudicative organs of the State.

*The general people's courts* are the Supreme People's Court and the local people's courts at different levels. There are four levels altogether. The presidents at each level are elected by the people's congresses at the corresponding levels, vice-presidents and general judges are subject to appointment by the standing committees of the people's congresses at corresponding levels.

*The special people's courts* are military courts, railway transportation courts and maritime courts.

Military courts include basic military courts, intermediate military courts and high military courts. They are competent to try criminal cases involving servicemen.

Railway transportation courts include basic railway transportation courts, intermediate railway transportation courts and high railway transportation courts. They are competent to try criminal and civil cases involving railway transportation.

Maritime courts exist only at the intermediate level. They are competent to try maritime cases.

There are two instances of trials: judgments or written orders of a court of first instance may be appealed to the court at the next higher level. The people's procuratorate may also protest the judgment before a court at the next higher level. If there is no appeal or protest within the designated

---

3 See Daniel C.K. Chow, The Legal System of the People's Republic of China in a Nutshell, Thomson West 2003, p. 195

period, judgments become legally effective[4]. Judgments of second instance and the decisions of the Supreme People's Court are final.

**2. Competence**

a. The Supreme People's Court

The Supreme People's Court is the highest adjudicative organ of the PRC. Its president (Chief Justice) is elected by the NPC and it is accountable to the NPC and the Standing Committee of the NPC. The term of office of the president of the Supreme People's Court is 5 years with a maximum of two consecutive terms. Vice-presidents and general judges are appointed and dismissed by the Standing Committee of the NPC.

The Supreme People's Court has the following chambers: chamber of putting cases on file (*li'an ting*), criminal chamber (*xingshi ting*), civil chamber (*minshi ting*), administrative chamber (*xingzheng ting*) and chamber of adjudicative supervision (*shenpan jiandu ting*).

One of the functions of the Supreme People's Court is supervision (not leadership) of the work of other courts (general or special courts at various levels).

Judicial interpretations of the Supreme People's Court are regarded as sources of law for the PRC.

b. High People's Courts

The high people's courts are of provincial level, *i.e.* in each of the 22 provinces, 5 autonomous regions and 4 municipalities directly under the central government there is a high people's court respectively. They are accountable to the

4 See Zhu Yikun, *China's Procedural Law*, Law Press China, Beijing 2003, pp. 8-9.

people's congresses and their standing committees at the provincial level. They supervise the work of the people's courts and maritime courts at lower levels.

c. Intermediate People's Courts

The intermediate people's courts are established in prefectures and municipalities at the prefectural level. They are accountable to the people's congresses and their standing committees at the prefectural level and supervise the work of the basic people's courts.

d. Basic People's Courts

Basic people's courts are established in counties, autonomous counties and districts of municipalities at the prefectural level. They are accountable to the people's congresses and their standing committees at county level. Cases in the first instance in civil, criminal and administrative matters are usually tried by basic people's courts.

Basic people's courts supervise the work of the people's mediation (conciliation) committees[5].

## C. People's Procuratorates

The people's procuratorates are State organs for legal supervision (Article 129 of the Constitution). The PRC establishes the Supreme People's Procuratorate and the local people's procuratorates at different levels, military procuratorates and other special people's procuratorates (Article 130 of the Constitution).

**1. Four Levels**

As far as the general people's procuratorates are con-

5 See Zhu Yikun, *China's Procedural Law*, Law Press China, Beijing 2003, pp. 9-11.

cerned, there are four levels altogether: the Supreme People's Procuratorate, people's procuratorates at the provincial level (provinces, autonomous regions and municipalities directly under the central government), branches of the people's procuratorates at the provincial level and the people's procuratorates in autonomous prefectures and provincially directed cities, as well as county and district people's procuratorates.

**2. Powers and Functions**

The powers and functions of the people's procuratorates include:

(a) exercising procuratorial power over treason cases, cases involving splitting the State and so on;

(b) investigating criminal cases, reviewing cases investigated by the public security organs, deciding whether to approve arrest, to prosecute or to exempt from prosecution;

(c) supervising the investigative activities of the public security organs;

(d) prosecuting criminal cases and supporting public prosecutions;

(e) supervising the adjudication activities of the people's courts;

(f) supervising the execution of judgments in criminal cases, activities of prisons, detention houses and the State organs in charge of reform-through-labor.

**3. The Supreme People's Procuratorate**

The Supreme People's Procuratorate is the highest procuratorial organ (Article 132, Paragraph 1 of the Constitution). It directs the work of the local people's procuratorates at different levels and of the special people's procuratorates (Article 132, Paragraph 1 of the Constitution). It is accountable to the NPC and the Standing Committee of the NPC. The Procurator-General is elected and may be

Procurator-General is elected and may be removed by the NPC, while deputy procurator-generals and general procurators are subject to appointment and dismissal by the Standing Committee of the NPC upon the nomination of the Procurator-General.

**4. Dual Leadership**

The people's procuratorates at lower levels than the Supreme People's Procuratorate are accountable not only to the people's congresses and their standing committees at the corresponding level, but also to the people's procuratorates at the next higher level. Therefore the local people's procuratorates are subject to dual leadership, *i.e.* to the leadership of the people's congresses as well as their standing committees at the corresponding level, and to the leadership of the people's procuratorates at the next higher level.[6]

**5. Judicial Interpretations Given by the Supreme People's Procuratorate**

Judicial interpretations given by the Supreme People's Procuratorate bind the procuratorial work of all the people's procuratorates. They constitute, at least in part, subsidiary sources of law of the PRC.

6 See Zhu Yikun, *China's Procedural Law*, Law Press China, Beijing 2003, pp. 11-13.

# Chapter Two An Overview of Chinese Civil Procedure

## I. Sources of Chinese Civil Procedural Law

The present code of civil procedure – the CPL of the PRC was adopted by the 4th Session of the Seventh NPC on 9 April 1991 and entered into effect on the same day.[1] It was amended in accordance with the "Decision of the Standing Committee of the NPC on Amending the CPL of the PRC" adopted by the 30th Session of the Standing Committee of the Tenth NPC of 28 October 2007. According to the Order of the President of the PRC (No. 75), the Decision on Amending the CPL of the PRC came into effect on 1 April 2008.

In China, judicial interpretations are documents issued by the Supreme People's Court and the Supreme People's Procuratorate in their adjudicative and procuratorial work.[2] According to Article 5 of the Provisions of the Supreme People's Court on the Work of Judicial Interpretations, which came into effect on 1 April 2007, judicial interpretations issued by the Supreme People's Court have force of law.

The Supreme People's Court issued the Opinions on Several Questions of Applying the CPL in 1992; in 2001,

---

1 Replacing the Civil Procedure Law (for trial implementation) adopted by the NPC in 1982.

2 See Daniel C.K. Chow, The Legal System of the People's Republic of China in a Nutshell, Thomson West 2003, pp. 167-170.

Some Provisions on Evidence for Civil Procedure were issued.

## II. Basic Principles of Chinese Civil Procedure

Articles 5-17 of the CPL set forth 14 basic principles of Chinese civil procedure:

**1. Court's Exclusive Exercise of Civil Adjudicative Power**

"The people's courts shall exercise the adjudicative powers with respect to civil cases." (Article 6 First Paragraph of the CPL)

**2. Court's Independent Trial**

"The people's courts shall try civil cases independently in accordance with the law, and shall be subject to no interference by any administrative organ, public organization or individual." (Article 6 Second Paragraph of the CPL)

This principle has already been embodied in Article 126 of the Constitution, which provides: "The people's courts shall, in accordance with the law, exercise adjudicative power independently and are not subject to interference by administrative organs, public organizations or individuals."

**3. Relying on the Facts and Taking the Law as the Criterion**

"In trying civil cases, the people's courts must base themselves on facts and take the law as the criterion." (Article 7 of the CPL)

**4. The Parties' Equal Litigation Rights**

"The parties in civil litigation shall have equal litigation rights." (Article 8 Sentence 1 of the CPL)

**5. Safeguarding and Facilitating the Parties' Exercise of Litigation Rights**

"The people's courts shall, in conducting the trials, safeguard their [the parties'] rights, facilitate their exercising the rights, and apply the law equally to them." (Article 8 Sentence 2 of the CPL)

**6. Equality and Reciprocity**

"Aliens, stateless persons, foreign enterprises and organizations that bring suits or enter appearance in the people's courts shall have the same litigation rights and obligations as citizens, legal persons and other organizations of the PRC.

If the courts of a foreign country impose restrictions on the civil litigation rights of the citizens, legal persons and other organizations of the PRC, the people's courts of the PRC shall follow the principle of reciprocity regarding the civil litigation rights of the citizens, enterprises and other organizations of that foreign country." (Article 5 of the CPL)

**7. Parties' Right to Use Native Languages**

"Citizens of all nationalities shall have the right to use their native spoken and written languages in civil proceedings." (Article 11 Paragraph 1 of the CPL)

**8. Right to Present Arguments**

"Parties to civil actions are entitled in the trials by the people's courts to argue for themselves." (Article 12 of the CPL)

## Case[3]

Company A and Company B jointly purchased items

---

[3] See Chen Guiming and Ma Huaide, Anli susongfa jiaocheng (*Teaching Manual of Procedural Law with Cases*), Vol. I, Beijing 1996, pp. 22-24.

from Company C. Something happened among them and A wanted to return the item bought from C, but C was opposed to this. Because the legal representative of B and that of C were relatives, A felt that both intended to infringe upon his rights and interests. Therefore he brought a lawsuit against B and C in a people's court. In the course of the proceedings, the legal representative of B argued that B should not be the defendant, since B and A had bought the object jointly from C. He thought B and A should have been co-plaintiffs. However, the chief judge said, "The matter of party is a matter of procedure. Since A sued B, the court has the power to decide the matter. Do not argue about such matters anymore." Question: is that reasonable?

Answer: in the instant case, B thought that it should not be the defendant. Its argument is based on a point of procedural law. Such an argument is founded in the litigation rights and should not be denied by the court.

**9. Freedom to Dispose of One's Civil and Litigation Rights**

"The parties are free to deal with their own civil rights and litigation rights the way they prefer within the scope provided by the law." (Article 13 of the CPL)

## Case[4]

In July 1993, the plaintiff A bought a machine from the defendant B for 160000 yuan RMB. Later, buyer A discovered a defect in the product and wanted to return the ma-

4 See Chen Guiming and Ma Huaide, Anli susongfa jiaocheng (*Teaching Manual of Procedural Law with Cases*), Vol. I, Beijing 1996, pp. 24-26.

chine to seller B, requesting a refund. B disagreed, and A launched a lawsuit in a people's court in October 1993. The court found that A was not at fault in the performance of the contract of sale, and the product manufactured and sold by B was defective in quality. Thus the defendant shall be held responsible in the sense of substantive law. During the proceeding, the plaintiff was aware of the fact that the defendant had been in financial difficulties and had ceased to manufacture products. Fearing that the defendant might not be able to repay, the plaintiff proposed that the machine would be returned to the defendant (the seller), and that only 130000 yuan RMB need to be repaid within one month. The defendant agreed and the two parties reached a settlement agreement.

In the instant case, the plaintiff partially gave up his own substantive claim, and reached an agreement with the defendant on a voluntary basis. This ought to be regarded as a disposal of civil and litigation rights within the scope provided by law. It should be approved by the people's court.

**10. Voluntary and Lawful Mediation**

"In trying civil cases, the people's courts shall conduct mediation for the parties on a voluntary and lawful basis; if mediation fails, judgments shall be rendered without delay." (Article 9 of the CPL)

"The people's mediation committee shall conduct mediation for the parties according to the law and on a voluntary basis. The parties concerned shall carry out the settlement agreement reached through mediation; those who decline mediation or those for whom mediation has failed or those who have backed out of the settlement agreement may institute legal proceedings in a people's court." (Article 16 Paragraph 2 of the CPL)

## Case[5]

B damaged a Sony video projector borrowed from A. A requested compensation of 10000 yuan RMB from B, but B refused to do so. A sued B in a people's court. The court tried many times to conciliate the dispute between the two parties. A maintained his claim of 10000 yuan RMB because the original product was available only in Japan whereas B only wanted to compensate 6000 yuan RMB at most, arguing that the product was already 2 years old. After several months B expressly declared to the court that he did not want to continue the mediation. The court thought that the two parties had been close friends and the object of dispute was not big. It maintained the mediation and postponed the judgment. After another four months, the plaintiff A protested to the court and requested a prompt judgment. The trial judge said to him, "It's quite easy for me to render a judgment, but it will be disadvantageous to you, for you might be compensated merely 5000 yuan RMB." Question: was that reasonable?

Answer: in the instant case, the court conducted mediation on an involuntary basis. It was wrong to do so, because any mediation conducted by a people's court shall be on the voluntary basis (Article 9 of the CPL).

5 See Chen Guiming and Ma Huaide, Anli susongfa jiaocheng (*Teaching Manual of Procedural Law with Cases*), Vol. I, Beijing 1996, pp. 14-18.

## Case[6]

Husband A and wife B married in 1985 and bore one daughter after the marriage. B instituted a lawsuit to a district people's court requesting divorce due to family violence. The court conciliated the dispute. A did not agree to divorce and did not want to support B and their daughter. B thought that the court might not approve the divorce; she was also concerned about the possible negative effects of divorce on their child. She said to the court that as long as A stopped the domestic violence, she would not divorce him and would accept the conditions set forth by A. The court made a protocol based on their agreement which was signed by both parties. OK?

In the instant case, the claim of A ignored the issue of support (maintenance) for B and their daughter. This was not in accordance with the principle of equality between men and women and the obligations of both parents to support their children. Thus the so-called mediation was not on a lawful basis. It should not be approved by the court (Article 9 of the CPL).

**11. Procuratorates' Supervision**

"The people's procuratorates shall have the right to exercise legal supervision over civil proceedings." (Article 14 of the CPL)

**12. Supporting the Injured Unit or Individual to Bring an Action**

"Where an act has infringed upon the civil rights and

---

[6] See Chen Guiming and Ma Huaide, Anli susongfa jiaocheng (*Teaching Manual of Procedural Law with Cases*), Vol. I, Beijing 1996, p. 19.

interests of the State, a collective organization or an individual, any State organ, public organization, enterprise or institution may support the injured unit or individual to bring an action in a people's court." (Article 15 of the CPL)

**13. People's Mediation**

"The people's mediation committees shall be mass organizations to conduct mediation of civil disputes under the guidance of the grass-roots level people's governments and the basic level people's courts." (Article 16 Paragraph 1 of the CPL).

Each urban neighborhood or village resident committee is entitled to establish a people's mediation committee. Each mediation committee consists of 3 to 9 members.[7]

**14. Making Supplementary Rules in Autonomous Regions**

"The people's congresses of the national autonomous regions may formulate, in accordance with the Constitution and the principles of this Law, and in conjunction with the specific circumstances of the local nationalities, adaptive and supplementary provisions." (Article 17 of the CPL).

## III. Basic Systems of Chinese Civil Procedure

"In trying civil cases, the people's courts shall, according to the provisions of the law, follow the systems of panel hearing, withdrawal, public trial and the court of second instance being that of last instance." (Article 10 of the CPL)

---

7 See Daniel C.K. Chow, The Legal System of the People's Republic of China in a Nutshell, Thomson West 2003, pp. 305-306.

## A. Panel Hearing System

### 1. Principle

In principle, it is the collegial panel with more than 3 adjudication officers which conducts the trial. But there are exceptions to this rule: a hearing before a single judge rather than a panel is permitted in the summary procedure applied by the basic people's courts and the tribunals dispatched by them when trying simple civil cases in which the facts are evident, the rights and obligations clear and the disputes trivial in character (Articles 142-146 of the CPL). Article 40 and Article 145 of the CPL specify that "civil cases in which summary procedure is followed shall be tried by a single judge alone", and "simple civil cases shall be tried by a single judge alone". In addition, cases tried in accordance with the special procedure provided for in Articles 160-176 shall be tried by a single judge alone (except for trials involving the qualification of voters or of major, difficult, or complicated cases, Article 161 of the CPL).

### 2. Structure

The collegial panel is composed of 3 or more adjudication officers. It must have an odd number of members. The collegial panel of first instance is composed either of both judges and adjudicative assessors, or of judges alone. When performing their duties, the adjudicative assessors have rights equal to those of the judges (Article 40 of the CPL). The collegial panel of second instance is composed of judges only (Article 41 of the CPL). However, for the collegial panel overseeing the retrial of a remanded case, the court of first instance shall form a new collegial panel in accordance with the procedure of first instance. If a case for retrial was originally tried at the first instance, a new

nally tried at the first instance, a new collegial panel shall be formed according to the procedure of first instance; if the case was originally tried at the second instance or was brought by a court at a higher level to the court of second instance for trial, a new collegial panel shall be formed according to the procedure of second instance (Article 41 of the CPL).

**3. Organization**

A judge shall be designated to serve as the presiding judge of the collegial panel; he is normally designated by the president of the court or the chief judge of a division. If the president or the chief judge of a division participates in the trial, he himself shall serve as the presiding judge (Article 42 of the CPL). Adjudicative assessors cannot serve as the presiding judge.[8]

When deliberating a case, a collegial panel shall observe the rule of majority (Article 43 of the CPL).

## B. Withdrawal System

**1. Aim**

The aim of the withdrawal system is to ensure procedural fairness or impartiality. It applies to the adjudication officers (judges or adjudicative assessors) as well as other relevant personnel *e.g.* clerks, interpreters, expert witnesses and inspection personnel.

**2. Statutory Causes**

Statutory causes of withdrawal may be as follows: (1) being a party to the case or a near relative of a party or an

---

8 See Zhu Yikun, *China's Procedural Law*, Law Press China, Beijing 2003, pp. 78-79.

agent *ad litem* in the case, *i.e.* spouse, parents, brothers and sisters, grandparents and grandchildren; (2) being an interested party in the case; (3) being someone with some other kind of relationship with a party to the case, which might affect the impartiality of the trial, *i.e.* other relatives or friends, former classmates (Article 45 of the CPL).

**3. Types**

There are two types of withdrawal: withdrawal by application and withdrawal on initiative. An application for withdrawal may be made orally or in writing. It may be submitted at the beginning of the proceedings or before the closing arguments in court.

**4. Decision**

The withdrawal of the court president serving as the presiding judge shall be decided on by the adjudication committee; the withdrawal of general adjudication officers shall be decided on by the court president; and the withdrawal of other personnel shall be decided on by the presiding judge (Article 47 of the CPL).

**5. Time**

The decision on an application for withdrawal shall be made within 3 days after the application was made (Article 48 of the CPL). At the beginning of a court session, the presiding judge shall ask the parties whether or not they wish to apply for the withdrawal of any court personnel (Article 123 of the CPL).

## C. Public Trial System

In principle, civil cases shall be tried in public. Exceptions to this rule are permitted where civil cases involve State secrets or personal privacy or are to be tried otherwise as provided by the law. Moreover, divorce cases and cases involving trade secrets may not be heard in public if a party so requests (Article 120 of the CPL).

If civil cases are to be tried in public, the names of the parties, the cause of action and the time and location of the court session shall be announced publicly (Article 123 of the CPL). Unless otherwise stipulated by law, citizens may observe the court session. Journalists may cover and report on the civil cases tried in public. The judgments rendered by the people's courts shall be announced publicly.[9]

## D. System of the Court of Second Instance Being That of the Last Instance

The party refusing to accept a judgment or written order of the first instance of a local people's court may file an appeal with the people's court at the next higher level (Article 147 of the CPL).

Judgments and written order made by the people's courts of second instance are final (Article 158 of the CPL). Decisions made by the Supreme People's Court are final.

Nevertheless, in cases tried in accordance with special procedure (*i.e.* cases concerning the qualification of voters, the declaration of a person as missing or dead, the determination of legal incapacity or restricted legal capacity of a citizen and the determination of a property as ownerless), the judgment of the first instance shall be final (Article 161 of the CPL).

---

9 See Zhang Weiping, Minshi susongfa (*Civil Procedural Law*), Law Press China, Beijing 2004, p. 73.

## Case[10]

The plaintiff A instituted a civil lawsuit against the defendant B before the people's court of a county. The people's court of first instance rendered a judgment according to which the defendant shall compensate the plaintiff 600 yuan RMB. The defendant appealed to the intermediate people's court of the prefecture against the judgment of the first instance.

The people's court of second instance upheld the facts certified by the court of first instance, and deemed the law applied correct. It refused the appeal and maintained the original judgment, declaring that the present judgment as final and not subject to appeal.

10 See Chen Guiming and Ma Huaide, Anli susongfa jiaocheng (*Teaching Manual of Procedural Law with Cases*), Vol. I, Beijing 1996, pp. 19-21.

# Chapter Three Court Competence and Court Jurisdiction in Civil Matters

## I. Court Competence in Civil Matters and Its Relationship to Mediation and Arbitration

### A. The Court Competence in Civil Matters

The court competence in civil matters refers to the authority of the people's courts to adjudicate civil cases. It relates to the distribution of power among the people's courts and other State organs (*e.g.* administrative agencies) as well as social organizations (*e.g.* the people's mediation committees).

**Case: Wang Chunli *et al.* versus Beijing Nationality Hotel[1]**

Wang Chunli and 15 others were employed by the defendant. According to Article 97, Paragraph 1 of the Constitution of the PRC citizens have the right to elect local representatives to the district people's congresses. In October 1998, the Beijing Nationality Hotel published a list of electorates. 16 people were on the list. However, due to the expiration of their labor contracts, the labor relationship between the co-plaintiffs and the defendant had been terminated. The Beijing Nationality Hotel did not inform the ex-employees of

---

1 Tang Weijian *et al.* (eds.), Minshi susongfa xue yuanli jiaocheng (*A Course in Principles and Cases of Science of Civil Procedure Law*), Renmin University Press, Beijing 2006, pp. 25-26.

their right to participate in the election and did not offer them an election certificate. As a result, the 16 ex-employees could not participate in the election. A lawsuit was filed in a people's court against the Beijing Nationality Hotel for infringing the right to election. The co-plaintiffs requested compensation in the amount of 2 million yuan RMB. The people's court found this matter being beyond the court competence since the issue was relating to the right to election and not the electorate qualification.

A written order was made by the people's court of the first instance. An appeal was filed. The people's court of the second instance rejected the appeal and upheld the initial written order.

## B. The Court Competence in Civil Matters and the Competence of the People's Mediation Committee

In areas where both a people's court and a people's mediation committee have the competence to decide a case, the competence of the people's mediation committee prevails, if both parties consent to mediation; the court competence prevails, if only one party applies for mediation, and the other party applies for litigation.

If the mediation fails or the parties dissolve their mediation agreement, the competence returns to the court.

## C. Court Competence and the Competence of Arbitration Institutions

### 1. General Principles

The competence of the people's courts is more extensive than that of arbitration institutions.

If the parties have concluded an arbitration agreement,

the competence of arbitration institutions prevails in shared areas.

If the arbitral award is nullified by the people's courts, then the competence is based on the parties' choice, *e.g.* if they reach an arbitration agreement, then only arbitration institutions are competent.

If the arbitration agreement is nullified by the people's courts, then only the people's courts are competent.

In labor disputes, the people's courts and labor dispute arbitration institutions have the same competence. But the people's courts may only adjudicate such cases after labor dispute arbitration institutions have done so.

**2. Arbitration as a Dispute Resolution Mechanism in China**

a. Arbitration Agreement

(1) Definition

An arbitration agreement is an agreement reached by the parties to submit their disputes to arbitration, whether or not administered by a permanent arbitral institution, all or certain disputes which have arisen or may arise between them in respect of a defined legal relationship, whether contractual or not.

(2) Two Types of Arbitration Agreements

There are two types of arbitration agreements: (i) a "submission to arbitration agreement", which takes the form of a separate contract, distinct from any contract from which the dispute arises; and (ii) an "arbitration clause", which is part of a substantive contract ("the matrix contract").[2]

[2] See Arzandeh and Hill, Ascertaining the Proper Law of an Arbitration Clause under English Law, in Journal of Private International Law, Vol. 5, No. 3, 2009, p. 427.

(3) Effect

An arbitration agreement excludes the competence of ordinary people's courts to decide on disputes arising within the subject matters.

(4) The Requirement of the Written Form

In China, an arbitration agreement has to be in writing.

(5) Reasons for Invalidity

According to Article 17 of the Arbitration Law, an arbitration agreement is invalid under any of the following circumstances:

a) the matters agreed for arbitration has exceeded the scope of arbitration provided by law;

b) the arbitration agreement has been concluded by a person who has no capacity to engage in civil juristic acts or who has restricted capacity to engage in civil juristic acts;

c) the arbitration agreement has been concluded by parties of which one forced upon the other by means of coercion.

(6) Principle of Autonomy or Separability of the Arbitration Clause

The arbitration agreement, especially the arbitration clause in a contract, should be treated as an agreement independent of other terms of the contract and of the contract itself.

b. Arbitrability

Article II, Paragraph 2 of the New York Convention on the Recognition and Enforcement of Foreign Judgments and Arbitral Awards of 1958 underlines that the Convention relates to differences arising from legal relationships "concerning a subject matter capable of settlement by arbitration."

## II. Court Jurisdiction

In China, the court jurisdiction in civil matters means the distribution of power of adjudicating civil cases of the first instance among the people's courts.

### A. Jurisdiction by Forum Level

Jurisdiction by forum level deals with the division of jurisdiction among the people's courts at various levels.

**1. Basic People's Courts**

Article 18 of the CPL stipulates: "The basic people's courts shall have jurisdiction as courts of first instance over civil cases, unless otherwise provided in this Law."

**2. Intermediate People's Courts**

According to Article 19 of the CPL, the intermediate people's courts shall have jurisdiction as courts of first instance over the following civil cases:

(1) major cases involving foreign elements;

(2) cases having major impact on the area under their jurisdiction;

(3) cases as determined by the Supreme People's Court to be under the jurisdiction of the intermediate people's courts.

**3. High People's Courts**

The high people's courts shall have jurisdiction as courts of first instance over civil cases having major impact on the areas at the provincial level (Article 20 of the CPL).

**4. Supreme People's Court**

The Supreme People's Court shall have jurisdiction as the court of first instance over the following civil cases (Article 21 of the CPL):

(1) cases having major impact on the whole country;

(2) cases that the Supreme People's Court deems it should try.

## B. Territorial Jurisdiction

### 1. General Territorial Jurisdiction

a. General Rule

A civil lawsuit brought against a citizen (or a legal person or any other organization) shall be under the jurisdiction of the people's court of the place where the defendant has his domicile; if the place of the defendant's domicile is different from that of his habitual residence, the lawsuit shall be under the jurisdiction of the people's court of the place of his habitual residence (Article 22 of the CPL).

#### Case[3]

Overseas Chinese Lin Tianmao was living in Malaysia with a Chinese nationality, but had no domicile in China. During a spring vacation he came back to China and did some shopping in a Beijing supermarket situated in Chaoyang District. He bought an electric shaver and took it to Malaysia. Because of a defect in the product the blade released and hurt his left eye (his vision went from 1.0 to 0.2). He brought a lawsuit against the supermarket in the No. 2 Intermediate People's Court in Beijing requesting 300000 yuan RMB.

In principle, civil cases should be tried at the basic level. Should the intermediate people's court be involved in the first instance?

---

[3] Ye Qing *et al.* (eds.), Minshi susongfa (*Civil Procedure Law*), Law Press China, Beijing 2006, pp. 19-22.

According to Article 1 of the Opinions of the Supreme People's Court issued in 1992 on Several Questions of Applying the CPL, "major" cases containing a foreign element are those cases containing a foreign element of which the objects are big or the circumstances are complicated or the parties living in foreign countries are numerous. They shall be under the jurisdiction of intermediate people's courts.

In the instant case of tort, the important things are the place of sale (China) and the place of injury (Malaysia). There is also the issue of the domicile of the defendant (China).

In this case the basic people's court has jurisdiction. However, if there were more foreign elements, more foreign plaintiffs or more complicated facts, the intermediate people's court would have jurisdiction.

## Case[4]

A man and a woman met through a matchmaker. The man sent the woman's parents several gifts. The couple broke up. Later, the man sued the woman and her parents in the people's court of the place where the co-defendants had their domicile. The woman and her parents argued that their domicile differed from their habitual residence. The man should have sued them at the place of habitual residence of the woman and her parents.

In the instant case, the co-defendants had their domicile in X, but the intermediate people's court nullified the decision of the basic people's court in X. Article 22 of the CPL declares that if the defendant's domicile is not the habitual resi-

4 Ye Qing *et al.* (eds.), Minshi susongfa (*Civil Procedure Law*), Law Press China, Beijing 2006, pp. 22-24.

dence, then the habitual residence takes precedence over the domicile. According to Article 5 of the Opinions of the Supreme People's Court issued in 1992 on Several Questions of Applying the CPL, the habitual residence is the place where a citizen constantly resides, starting from the time he leaves his domicile, to the time of launching the lawsuit. This period must be at least 1 year, unless it is the place where one receives medical treatment. In the instant case the co-defendants had a habitual residence for longer than 1 year.

### Case

A man and a woman married in 1992. Both had earlier marriages. The wife had a son and the husband had 2 daughters. He died. She made phone calls requesting that her son and her 2 step-daughters shall pay her maintenance fee. Since they did not react, she brought a lawsuit. The mother lived in district A. The children lived in districts B, C and D. One daughter lived in district D and worked in district E.

The people's court of which district shall have jurisdiction?

Generally speaking, the people's court of the district in which the defendant has his domicile shall have territorial jurisdiction (Article 22 of the CPL). However, in this case there were multiple co-defendants. Thus, the people's courts of districts B, C, D or E might respectively refuse to hear the case, as the court would only have jurisdiction over one of the co-defendants. In this case the plaintiff might bring the lawsuit to the people's court in district A.

Article 9 of the Opinions of the Supreme People's Court issued in 1992 on Several Questions of Applying the CPL: if the domiciles of several defendants in cases of requesting alimony are in various areas, the people's court at the plaintiff's domicile may have jurisdiction.

b. Exceptions to the Rule

The following civil lawsuits shall be under the jurisdiction of the people's court of the place where the plaintiff has his domicile/habitual residence (Article 23 of the CPL):

a) civil lawsuits concerning personal status brought against persons not residing within the PRC;

b) civil lawsuits concerning the personal status of persons whose whereabouts are unknown or who have been declared as missing;

c) civil lawsuits brought against persons who are undergoing rehabilitation through labor; and

d) civil lawsuits brought against persons who are in prison.

**2. Special Territorial Jurisdiction**

In some cases there may exist special territorial jurisdiction of a certain people's court. Those cases are the following:

(1) A lawsuit on a contract dispute: the defendant's domicile or the place of performance (Article 24 of the CPL);

(2) A lawsuit on an insurance contract dispute: the defendant's domicile or location of the insured object (Article 26 of the CPL);

(3) A lawsuit on a bill dispute: the place of payment of the bill or the defendant's domicile (Article 27 of the CPL);

(4) A lawsuit on a dispute over a railway, road, water or air transport contract/a dispute over a combined transport contract: the place of dispatch or the place of destination or the defendant's domicile (Article 28 of the CPL);

(5) A lawsuit on a tortious act: the place of the commission of the tortious act or the defendant's domicile (Article 29

of the CPL);

(6) A lawsuit on claims for damages caused by a railway, road, or water transport or by an air accident: the place of accident, the place of the vehicle or ship's first arrival, the place of the aircraft's first landing or the defendant's domicile (Article 30 of the CPL);

(7) A lawsuit on claims for damages caused by a collision at sea or by any other maritime accident: the place where the collision occurred, the place where the ship in collision first docked after the accident or where the ship at fault was detained, or the defendant's domicile (Article 31 of the CPL);

(8) A lawsuit on expenses of maritime salvage: the place where the salvage took place, the place where the salvaged ship first docked after the disaster (but not the place of the defendant's domicile, Article 32 of the CPL);

(9) A lawsuit on general average: the place where the ship first docked or where the adjustment of general average was conducted or where the voyage ended (but not the place of the defendant's domicile, Article 33 of the CPL).

### Case

A sold a piece of calligraphy to B for 100000 yuan RMB, to be paid in city Y. A and B are in city X, and the contract was made in X. A changed his mind later and claimed that he had sold the calligraphy to D. B sued A. Which court had jurisdiction?

It was a contractual dispute, so Article 24 of the CPL must be taken into consideration.

Article 18 of the Opinions of the Supreme People's Court issued in 1992 on Several Questions of Applying the CPL is actually a supplement to the CPL. According to Article 18 of this judicial interpretation, if the contract has not actually been performed, and the domiciles of the parties are not at the place of performance as agreed in the contract, then the people's court at the defendant's domicile alone shall have jurisdiction.

Our case deals with a contract of sale. Where was the place of performance? It was the place of "selling", *i.e.* the place where the property title was transferred. If A sells to B in Beijing, with money to be paid in Shanghai, then the place of performance is in Beijing. Thus, in this case, the court in district X had jurisdiction.

## C. Exclusive Jurisdiction (Article 34 of the CPL)

A lawsuit brought on the following disputes shall be under the exclusive jurisdiction of the people's courts:

(1) on a dispute over a real estate: the people's courts at the location of the real estate;

(2) on a dispute over harbor operations: the people's courts at the location of the harbor;

(3) on a dispute over succession: the people's courts at the place of where the deceased had his last domicile upon his death, or where the principal part of his estate is located.

### Case[5]

Zhang Hao and Zhang Huaili are husband and wife. They are residents of No. 82 of Laoshan Hutong, Dongcheng District, Beijing Municipality. In July 1993, a construction corporation based in Xicheng District sent some workers to the residence of the couple to repair the house before the

5 Ye Qing *et al.* (eds.), Minshi susongfa (*Civil Procedure Law*), Law Press China, Beijing 2006, pp. 30-31.

rainy season. During the project, workers repaired the house and renovated a wall. A worker became friend with the two landlords. One day, after work hours, the worker was invited by the landlords for dinner. As he left the house, he carelessly caused damage to the color TV. After the project had been finished, during the rainy season, the co-plaintiffs found that the wall had been damaged from rain. The whole house had water damage. It was uninhabitable. Later, the couple got divorced. According to the divorce agreement, each of the spouses should get one room. On 20 May 1995, Mr. Zhang Hao asserted that the construction corporation had caused serious damages during the renovation, had used defective products, and had also caused damage to the TV. The ex-wife Zhang Huaili also filed a lawsuit on the same cause of action. The Xicheng District People's Court of Beijing Municipality combined the two cases. The parties lived in Dongcheng District.

Which people's court had jurisdiction?

According to Article 34 Paragraph 1 of the CPL, a dispute arising from real estate shall be under the exclusive jurisdiction of the people's court at the location of the real estate, which will prevail even if the parties otherwise submitted the case for trial. Thus the people's court in Dongcheng District had jurisdiction, not the people's court in Xicheng District.

## D. Consensual Jurisdiction

### 1. Meaning

The parties may, under the statutory conditions, agree to choose the people's court exercising jurisdiction over their civil case (Article 25 and Article 242 of the CPL).

**2. Applicable Scope**

(1) contractual disputes in purely domestic cases (Article 25 of the CPL);

(2) contractual and property disputes involving foreign elements (Article 242 of the CPL).

**3. Written Form**

An agreement on the court jurisdiction must be in written form.

**4. First Instance Only**

The consensual jurisdiction is only permitted in civil cases of first instance.

**5. Limitations on Choice**

The chosen courts must somehow otherwise meet the statutory jurisdictional requirements for purely domestic cases, *e.g.* it must be at the place of the defendant's domicile, the place of contract performance or contract signature, the place of the plaintiff's domicile, or the place of the object of the action (Sentence 1 of Article 242 of the CPL).

For contract and property disputes involving foreign elements, the chosen courts must be courts having a practical connection with the case.

**6. Preconditions**

The provisions of the CPL regarding the jurisdiction by forum level and the exclusive jurisdiction shall not be violated.

## E. Transfer of Jurisdiction

If a people's court finds that a case it has accepted is not within its jurisdiction, it shall refer the case to the people's court that has jurisdiction. The people's court to which a case has been referred shall accept the case, unless it considers that the case referred to it is not within its jurisdiction. In that situation, the court shall report to a superior people's court for a designation of jurisdiction (Article 36 of the CPL).

### Case: Dong versus Company A and Company B for Product Liability[6]

The plaintiff Mr. Dong bought many bottles of beer from Company A whose seat was in District E of a city. The beer was manufactured by Company B whose seat was in District F of the same city. The plaintiff celebrated with his colleagues and friends in District C of the same city. One of the bottles exploded and damaged the eye of the plaintiff. The plaintiff brought a lawsuit in the people's court of District C, and then brought a lawsuit in the people's court of District E (at the seller's seat) and requested that the court should render a judgment which makes company A (the seller) and Company B (the manufacturer) jointly liable for expenses for medical care, travel costs and spiritual compensation.

Two people's courts in districts C and E accepted the cases. However, the people's court in District E transferred the case to District C. Was this correct?

*In casu*, District C was the place of commission of the tortious act, District E was the place of sale. According to Article 29 of the Opinions of the Supreme People's Court issued in 1992 on Several Questions of Applying the CPL, a lawsuit concerning the damage of property or personal injury

---

6 Tang Weijian *et al.* (eds.), Minshi susongfa xue yuanli jiaocheng (*A Course in Principles and Cases of Science of Civil Procedure Law*), Renmin University Press, Beijing 2006, pp. 133-134.

of another person having resulted from bad quality of products shall be under the jurisdiction of the people's court where the products have been manufactured, the place where the products were sold, the place where the tortious act was committed or the domicile of the defendant. The people's court in District E was aware of the fact that the people's court in District C had accepted the case. It was correct for the people's court in District E to make a written order to transfer jurisdiction to the people's court in District C (Article 35 of the CPL).

## F. Designation of Jurisdiction

If a people's court having jurisdiction over a civil case is unable to exercise the jurisdiction for special reasons, a superior people's court shall designate another court to exercise jurisdiction. In the event of a jurisdictional dispute between two or more people's courts, it shall be resolved by the disputing parties through consultation; if the dispute cannot be so resolved, it shall be reported to their common superior people's court for the designation of jurisdiction (Article 37 of the CPL).

## G. Objection of Jurisdiction

If a party to an action objects to the jurisdiction of a people's court after the court has entertained the case, the party must raise the objection within the period prescribed for the submission of defense. If the objection is established, the peoples court shall order the case to be transferred to the people's court that has jurisdiction over it; if not, the people's court shall reject the case (Article 38 of the CPL).

## Case: Zhang versus Li[7]

Zhang got to know Li in County B in 1995. They lived with each other in County A starting from 1996. Both were married at that time. In 1997, they conducted business together. Li helped Zhang and Zhang lent 100000 yuan RMB to Li in 1999. Both agreed that the money should be returned by 31 December 2001. In December 1999 they split up. Zhang filed a lawsuit in County C, the domicile of the defendant, requesting the return of the lent money. Li argued that she had left County C and migrated to County D and that her actual habitual residence was now County D. She had left County C 8 years ago (recall that the time needed to establish a habitual residence is 1 year). Nevertheless, the people's court in County C made a written order and rejected Li's objection. How could Li respond to this rejection?

Li could file an appeal to the people's court at the next higher level within 10 days of the rejection of her objection (Article147 Paragraph 2 of the CPL). She did so. The people's court of second instance made a final written order and annulled the written order made by the people's court of first instance. The case was finally transferred to the competent people's court in County D. Was this correct?

*In casu*, the domicile of the defendant Li was in County C, and her habitual residence was in County D. According to Article 22 Paragraph 1 of the CPL, if the place of the defendant's domicile is different from that of his habitual residence,

---

[7] Tang Weijian *et al.* (eds.), Minshi susongfa xue yuanli jiaocheng (*A Course in Principles and Cases of Science of Civil Procedure Law*), Renmin University Press, Beijing 2006, pp. 153.

the civil lawsuit shall be under the jurisdiction of the people's court at the place of his habitual residence. The people's court in County D should have jurisdiction. It was correct for the people's court of second instance to make a final written order leading to the transfer of jurisdiction from the people's court in District C to the people's court in District D.

### Case: Jinan Factory versus Nanjing Company[8]

In May 1998, a chemistry plant in Jinan (hereinafter referred to as "Jinan Factory") based in District A, Jinan City, signed a contract of sale with a chemical products company in Nanjing (hereinafter referred to as "Nanjing Company"), based in District B, Nanjing City. The contract of sale was signed in Wuxi, Jiangsu Province. It was agreed that Jinan Factory should send 30 tons of chemical and industrial raw materials to the Nanjing Company three times between July 1998 and December 1998. The price would be paid upon arrival of the products. In July 1998, Jinan Factory sent the first shipment of products (10 tons) to Nanjing Company and received 300000 yuan RMB in return. But the market price went up in August, and Jinan Factory stopped sending products to Nanjing Company. Nanjing Company's production suffered losses due to the lack of raw materials. Repeated requests didn't produce any results. Nanjing Company turned to another chemistry plant in Shanghai and bought 20 tons of chemical and industrial raw materials at a higher price. In September 1998, the price of chemical and industrial raw materials went down. Jinan Factory continued to send products

8 Ye Qing *et al.* (eds.), Minshi susongfa (*Civil Procedure Law*), Law Press China, Beijing 2006, pp. 45-48.

to Nanjing Company even though Nanjing Company had withdrawn from the contract of sale. Jinan Factory argued that the contract of sale had not specified a concrete time of performance. The products arrived in Nanjing and Nanjing Company refused them, and sent them to a company making chemical products in Wuhan. In Anqing, the ship of the carrier, a transportation company in Nanjing, collided with a ship from Chongqing. Some chemical and industrial raw materials leaked into the Yangtze River causing pollution. In October 1998, Jinan Factory urged Nanjing Company to pay the price for the material. In October 1998, Jinan Factory filed a lawsuit in the people's court of District A, Jinan City, requesting Nanjing Company to assume liability for breach of contract. Having received the complaint, the people's court of District A, Jinan City, sent notice for appearance in court and a copy of the complaint to the defendant Nanjing Company. The defendant raised an objection against the jurisdiction of the people's court of District A, Jinan City, and argued that the litigation should be under the jurisdiction of the people's court of District B, Nanjing City.

Objection based on special jurisdiction – this is about a contractual issue. Where was the contract performed? In a delivery contract, it is the place of delivery. According to Article 24 of the CPL, a contract is under the jurisdiction of either the defendant's domicile or the place where the contract is performed. Thus, the lawsuit could only be filed in district B, Nanjing City, as this is both the defendant's domicile and the place of performance.

# Chapter Four Litigation Participants

## I. Parties

### A. The Plaintiff and the Defendant and Their Rights and Obligations

**1. Principle**

Any citizens, legal persons and any other organization may become parties to a civil action (Article 49 of the CPL), *i.e.* the plaintiffs and the defendants.

Legal persons shall be represented by their legal representatives in the litigation. Other organizations shall be represented by their principal heads in the proceedings.

**2. Rights of the Parties to a Civil Action**

Parties to a civil action shall have the following rights: a) the right to appoint agents, apply for withdrawals, collect and provide evidence, proffer arguments, request mediation, file an appeal and apply for execution (Article 50 Paragraph 1 of the CPL); b) the right to have access to materials pertaining to the case and make copies thereof and other legal documents pertaining to the case (Article 50 Paragraph 2 of the CPL); c) the right to reach a compromise of their own accord (Article 51 of the CPL); d) (for the plaintiff) the right to relinquish or modify his claims, (for the defendant) the right to admit or rebut the claims as well as the right to file counterclaims.

**3. Obligations of the Parties to a Civil Action**

The obligations of the parties to a civil action are the following: the obligation to exercise their litigation rights in accordance with the law, the obligation to observe the procedures, and the obligation to carry out legally effective written judgments or orders as well as mediation statements (Article 50 Paragraph 3 of the CPL).

### Case: Yao versus Wang for Tort

On the way home after school, Wang (an 8-year-old boy) pushed Yao (a 7-year-old girl) and Yao fell and hit her head on a stone on the ground. This caused injury to Yao's body. Expenses for medical care and nourishment arose for Yao. But Yao's father and Wang's father were in dispute. Could Yao file a lawsuit against Wang in a people's court?

According to Article 49 of the CPL, any citizen, legal person and other organization may become parties to a civil action. Even though Yao and Wang were minors, they had the litigation right to sue and can be sued. So Yao could file a lawsuit against Wang in a people's court.

Nevertheless, both the plaintiff Yao and the defendant Wang did not have the capacity to act on their own in the litigation. Their parents had to represent them in the litigation in the capacity of an agent *ad litem*.

## B. Parties to a Joint Action

### 1. Prerequisites of a Joint Action

An action is a joint action if

a) one party or both parties consist of two or more than two persons, or

b) their object of action is the same or of the same category, and the people's court considers that, with the consent of the parties, the action can be tried in a combined way (see Article 53 Paragraph 1 of the CPL).

## Case: Intestate Succession of Brothers of Family Qi[1]

After the death of the old man Mr. Qi, his 7 sons got involved in a dispute over the succession of his property. A lawsuit was filed in a people's court. The youngest brother Qi 7 sued the oldest brother Qi 1 for infringing his inheritance right. After having entertained the case, the people's court informed the other 5 sons to appear in court. Qi 3 and Qi 4 expressly waived their substantive rights and did not participate in the litigation. Qi 2 and Q 5 said nothing, while Qi 6 was willing to participate in the litigation. Who shall be the plaintiff?

According to Article 54 and Article 58 of the Opinions of the Supreme People's Court issued in 1992 on Several Questions of Applying the CPL, if one of the successors files a lawsuit in an inheritance litigation, the people's court shall inform the other successors of their right to participate in the litigation as joint plaintiffs. Those successors who have been informed but are not willing to participate in the litigation and have not expressly waived their substantive rights, shall still be joint plaintiffs; their non-appearance in court shall not influence the trial and judgment of the court.

In the instant case, Qi 7, Qi 6, Qi 2 and Qi 5 shall be joint plaintiffs. The non-appearance of Qi 3 and Q 4 should not influence the trial.

**2. Effects on Persons Forming a Party to a Joint Action**

If two or more persons forming a party to a joint action

---

[1] Question raised by the Examination of the Lawyer's Qualification of 2000.

have common rights and obligations with respect to the object of action and the act of anyone of them is recognized by the others of the party, such an act shall be valid for all the rest of the party; if they have no common rights and obligations with respect to the object of action, the act of anyone of them shall not be valid for the rest (Article 53 Paragraph 2 of the CPL).

### Case: Who Was the Plaintiff and Who Was the Defendant?

Wang, Lu, and Li were all residents of District P of City H. One day they were drinking beer at Wang's house, at Wang's invitation. One beer bottle shattered and the glass hurt Wang, Lu, and Li in various degrees. They were sent to the hospital immediately. After having left the hospital, Wang went to the grocery store which had sold the beer. The store used the business license of Food Company Y of City H. The grocery store sent employees to investigate at Wang's house and found that the beer had really been sold by the grocery store itself and held that the accident had been caused by quality problems of the beer bottle. The grocery store argued that the beer manufacturing factory, whose seat is located in City A of a neighboring province, should be responsible. The grocery store refused to compensate.

Wang, Lu and Li decided to sue – who was the plaintiff and who was the defendant?

Was the defendant the beer manufacturing factory or the grocery? Or the food company the business licence of which the grocery used? Or both?

Wang, Lu, and Li could be co-plaintiffs and they might sue both the beer manufacturing factory and the holding food company of the grocery. Could they also sue the grocery? Yes, they could. But the grocery might claim from the owning food company (Article 41 of the Opinions of the Supreme People's Court issued in 1992 on Several Questions of Applying the CPL).

## C. Representatives of a Party

### 1. Representatives of a Party to a Joint Action (Article 54 of the CPL)

If the persons forming a party to a joint action are large in number, the party may elect representatives from among themselves to act for them in the litigation. The acts of such representatives in the litigation are valid for every member of the party they represent.

Exceptionally, the following matters shall be subject to the consent of the members of the party they represent: a) modification or waiver of claims; b) admission of the claims of the other party or c) pursuit of a compromise with the other party.

### 2. Representatives of Those Who Registered Their Rights with the Court

(1) Conditions

If the object of action is of the same category, and the persons forming one of the parties are large but uncertain in number at the commencement of the action, the people's court may issue a public notice, stating the particulars and claims of the case and informing those entitled to participate in the action to register their rights with the people's court within a fixed period of time (Article 55 Paragraph 1 of the CPL).

(2) Ways of Becoming Representatives

The representatives may be elected by those who have registered their rights with the people's court, or determined by the court through consultation with those who have registered their rights with the court (Article 55 Paragraph 2 of the CPL).

(3) Effects

In principle, the acts of the representatives in the litigation are valid for the party they represent. Exceptionally, modification or waiver of claims or admission of the claims of the other party or pursuit of a compromise with the other party shall be subject to the consent of the members of the party they represent.

The judgments or written orders rendered by the people's court shall be valid for all those who have registered their rights with the court (Article 55 Paragraph 4 of the CPL).

### Case: Passengers versus the Airline Company

A flight from Hainan to Beijing was canceled. 236 tickets had been sold for this flight. Passengers brought a lawsuit against the airline company in a people's court. The people's court received the case and issued a public notice. 202 passengers registered their rights with the people's court. They elected A, B and C as representatives in the litigation. The People's Court tried mediation between the parties on a voluntary basis. A, B and C reached a settlement agreement with the airline company, according to which the airline company would issue a public apology as well as small souvenirs to the passengers. The ticket price would also be refunded.

According to Article 55 Paragraph 3 of the CPL, the acts

of the representatives A, B, and C in the litigation are valid for the party they represent. The rest of the passengers must accept the result.

## D. Third Party (Article 56 of the CPL)

A third party who considers that he has an independent claim to the object of action of both parties shall have the right to bring an action.

A third party having no independent claim to the object of action of both parties may, if the outcome of the case will affect his legal interests, file a request to participate in the proceedings or the people's court shall notify him to participate.

A third party that is to bear civil liability in accordance with the judgment of the people's court shall be entitled to the rights and obligations of a party in litigation.

### Case: Lu versus Liu

Mr. Liu and Mr. Lu signed a contract of sale, in which Liu sold an apartment to Lu for 450000 yuan RMB. After some time, Lu found that the quality of the apartment was seriously defective. Lu filed a lawsuit against Liu in a people's court for serious defects in the apartment.

Yu believed that he had an ownership interest in the apartment. He went to the people's court and requested to participate in the litigation.

Question 1: How should the people's court adjudicate this matter?

Question 2: Assume that the apartment sold by Liu had been purchased from Yu one month ago, and Yu feels that his interests might be involved in the lawsuit. What can he do?[2]

Answer: in question 1, Yu was a third party with an independent claim. He might either participate in the litigation between Liu and Lu or institute another lawsuit against Liu and Lu. In question 2, Yu was a third party without an independent claim. If the outcome of the case affected his legal interest, he might file a request to participate in the proceedings or the people's court had to notify him, giving him the option of participating in the proceedings (Article 56 of the CPL).

## II. Agents *ad Litem*

### A. Statutory Agent and Appointed Agent *ad Litem*

#### 1. Statutory Agent

The guardian or guardians of any person of no capacity to engage in litigation may be designated statutory agents able to act for him and engage in litigation. If the statutory agents try to shift responsibility as agents *ad litem* upon one another, the people's court shall appoint one of them to represent the person in litigation (Article 57 of the CPL).

**Case: Lin versus Zhou for Personal Injury[3]**

Zhou (5-year-old boy) went to a park with his grandmother on a Sunday. During a game Zhou hurt the 6-year-old girl Lin causing blindness of Lin's right eye and eyesight decrease of the left eye. The father of Lin requested family

---

2 See Ye Qing *et al.* (eds.), Minshi susongfa (*Civil Procedure Law*), Law Press China, Beijing 2006, pp. 91-92.

3 Question raised in the unified National Judicial Exam of 2002.

Zhou to compensate the loss suffered by Lin, altogether 60000 yuan RMB. The father of Zhou refused to compensate on the ground that Zhou was not adult. Family Lin wanted to file a lawsuit in a people's court. Who shall be the litigation participants?

According to Article 57 of the CPL, persons of no capacity to engage in litigations shall be represented in the proceedings by their guardians who act as legal representatives. In the instant case, the plaintiff was Lin, represented by her father; the defendant was Zhou, represented by his father, whereas his grandmother was a witness. Nevertheless, it was the guardians who assume responsibility in case of injuries caused by persons of no or limited capacity to engage in civil juristic acts (Article 133 of the General Principles of Civil Law of the PRC). Therefore, the litigation participant may be different from the subject assuming civil liability.

**2. Appointed Agent *ad Litem***

A party to an action or a statutory agent may appoint one or two persons to act as his agents *ad litem*. A lawyer, a near relative, a unit to which the party belongs, or any other citizen approved by the people's court may be appointed as the party's agent *ad litem* (Article 58 of the CPL).

## B. Power of Attorney (Article 59 of the CPL)

The power of attorney must be submitted to the people's court by the principal. It must specify the matters entrusted and the powers conferred to the agent *ad litem*.

Special powers must be obtained by an agent *ad litem* from his principal to admit, waive or modify claims, to compromise, or to file a counterclaim or an appeal.

### Case

Lao Ma wanted to file a lawsuit. He went to a law firm named Dongfang and hired Attorney Zhuang to be his lawyer by signing a mandate contract with the latter. As to the power of attorney, the contract provided only "general agency". Several months later, when Lao Ma went to the court inquiring about the progress of his litigation, he was informed that Attorney Zhuang had waived the claim in his name. Lao Ma asked the court why it allowed Attorney Zhuang to withdraw the case. The judge replied that the mandate contract allowed "general agency", meaning that the mandated lawyer was empowered to represent Lao Ma in all litigation activities, including withdrawing the case. What are our comments on what the lawyer and the judge have done in the case?

According to Article 59 of the CPL, the power of attorney must specify the matters entrusted and the powers conferred – a general mandate is impossible. Special powers must be obtained by an agent *ad litem* from his principal to admit, waive or modify claims, or to compromise or to file a counterclaim or an appeal. Article 69 of the Opinions of the Supreme People's Court issued in 1992 on Several Questions of Applying the CPL: If the power of attorney merely mentions "general agency" without specifying the concrete matters, then the agent *ad litem* is not entitled to admit, waive or modify claims, or to compromise or to file a counterclaim or an appeal in lieu of the principal.

## C. Change or Revocation of the Powers of an Agent *ad Litem*

A party to an action shall inform the court in writing if he changes or revokes the powers of an agent *ad litem*. The court shall notify the other party of the change or revocation (Article 60 of the CPL).

### D. Rights of a Lawyer Serving as an Agent *ad Litem* and other Agents *ad Litem*

A lawyer who serves as an agent *ad litem* and other agents *ad litem* shall have the right to investigate and collect evidence, and the right to have access to materials pertaining to the case (Article 61 of the CPL).

### E. Exception: Divorce Cases

In divorce cases, where the parties are represented by their agents ad litem, they shall still appear in court in person, unless they are incapable of expressing their own will. A party who is truly unable to appear in court due to a special reason shall submit his views in writing to the people's court (Article 61 of the CPL).

#### Case: Li versus Wang for Divorce[4]

Li and Wang registered to marry in 1990. They got along well after the marriage. In June 2002, Li went on a trip for business. He was struck by a car in a traffic accident. Though he received medical treatment, he could not care for himself. He was identified as a person without capacity to engage in civil acts. After the New Year's Day of 2004, the mother of Li, Madame Cai found that her daughter-in-law Wang left home early and returned lately, without caring for Li and family affairs. Cai suspected Wang to have a lover. Cai filed a lawsuit

---

[4] See Tang Weijian *et al.* (eds.), Minshi susongfa xue yuanli jiaocheng (*A Course in Principles and Cases of Science of Civil Procedure Law*), Renmin University Press, Beijing 2006, p. 182.

in the name of Li in a people's court, requesting divorce with Wang. What are your comments?

The key point of the present case is whether a person of no capacity may act as the plaintiff in a divorce case. Firstly, a petition of divorce shall be raised by a party in person. No third person (including the agent *ad litem*) may make a declaration as to the consent to dissolve the marriage. Secondly, a person of no capacity may not act as plaintiff in divorce litigation. Thirdly, so long as Wang didn't give up her status as legal representative, Cai could not represent Li, because the spouse is the statutory guardian of first order, whereas parents are of second order. In a word, Wang could not be sued in a divorce case.

# Chapter Five Evidence

## I. General Principles

### A. Main Sources

There are two main sources of evidence in Chinese CPL: Articles 63-74 of the CPL of 1991 and the Rules of Evidence for Civil Procedure (Evidence Rules) issued by the Supreme People's Court on 12 December 2002.

### B. Classification of Evidence (Article 63 Paragraph 1 of the CPL)

(1) Documentary Evidence;
(2) Material Evidence;
(3) Audio-Visual Material;
(4) Testimony of Witnesses;
(5) Statements of the Parties;
(6) Expert Conclusions; and
(7) Records of Inspection.

The above-mentioned evidence must be verified before it can be taken as a basis for ascertaining a fact (Article 63 Paragraph 2 of the CPL).

#### Case[1]

A construction corporation incautiously struck a gable of a private residence nearby during a construction. Several

---

[1] See Ye Qing *et al.* (eds.), Minshi susongfa (*Civil Procedure Law*), Law Press China, Beijing 2006, pp. 100-102.

pieces of furniture and electrical appliances were damaged. When the accident took place, the 60-year-old resident Zhao was inside the building. Being scared, he was fleeing in a hurry and hurt his leg. The two parties could not reach an agreement as to the amount of compensation. Zhao filed a lawsuit in a people's court and submitted the following pieces of evidence: (1) the written record made by Zhao himself about what had happened; (2) tape and video cassettes made by a journalist of a local television station; (3) some photos of damaged things at the scene of accident; (4) a contract concluded by Zhao and a decoration company 3 months ago to fit up the house, the receipt of payment, and testimony made by Zhu, the responsible person of the decoration company; (5) material objects of a damaged microwave and a damaged TV set; (6) a medical certificate about the wound on Zhao's leg as well as payment receipts for medical treatment; (7) testimony of Madame Wang of the residents' committee after hearing Zhao's statement; (8) statements of some onlookers on the scene of accident.

The defendant also submitted evidence when handing over the complaint: some photos taken by the defendant at the scene of accident, photos showing that there were no falling objects caused by the collapse of the gable near the microwave and TV set (to explain that their damages were not caused by the collapse of the gable); photos taken by the defendant showing the renovation of the gable on the day of accident, as well as a news report that appeared in a local evening paper on the same day. What types of evidence have been submitted here?

In the instant case, the contract concluded by Zhao and the decoration company to fit up the house, the payment receipt as well as the payment receipts for the medical treatment are to be considered documentary evidence; the photos taken by the plaintiff and the defendant, as well as material objects of the microwave and the TV set are to be considered material evidence; the testimony made by Zhu, the medical certificate about the wound of Zhao's leg, the testimony of Madame Wang, the statements of the onlookers and the report of the local evening newspaper are to be considered testimony of witnesses; the written record made by Zhao himself about the incident is to be considered the statement of party.

## II. Burden of Proof and the Court's Right to Investigate and Collect Evidence

### A. Burden of Proof

It is the duty of a party to an action to provide evidence in support of his aggregation (Article 64 of the CPL).

The people's court shall investigate and collect evidence under one of the following conditions: (1) a party and, if applicable, his agent *ad litem* are unable to collect the evidence by themselves for objective reasons, or (2) the people's court considers the evidence necessary for the trial of the case.

In principle, evidence shall be presented in court and cross-examined by the parties concerned (Article 66 of the CPL). But there are exceptions to the rule, *e.g.* evidence involving State secrets, trade secrets and personal privacy shall be kept confidential.

### B. Right of the Court to Make Investigation and Collect Evidence (Article 65 of the CPL)

The people's court has the right to investigate and collect evidence from the relevant units or individuals; such units or individuals may not refuse to provide information and evidence.

The court shall verify the authenticity, examine and determine the validity of the certifying documents provided by the relevant units or individuals.

## III. Originality of Evidence (Article 68 of the CPL)

In principle, any document submitted as evidence must be the original. Material evidence must also be original.

But there are exceptions to the rule: reproductions, photographs, duplicates or extracts of the original may be submitted if it is truly difficult to present the original document or thing.

If a document in a foreign language is submitted as evidence, a Chinese translation must be appended.

## IV. Expert Evaluation (Article 72 of the CPL)

The prerequisite for an expert evaluation is that the people's court deems it necessary to make an expert evaluation of a problem of technical nature.

The people's court shall refer the problem to an authorized department or one department appointed by it.

A written conclusion of the evaluation duly sealed or

signed shall be presented by the authorized department and the experts.

## V. Inspection (Article 73 of the CPL)

Material evidence or a site may be inspected by the inspector.

The party concerned or an adult member of his family shall be present.

A written record of the circumstances and results of the inspection shall be made by the inspector.

## VI. Preservation of the Evidence (Article 74 of the CPL)

If it is likely that evidence may be destroyed or lost, or difficult to obtain later, the participants in the proceedings may apply to the people's court for preservation of the evidence. The people's court may also take measures on its own initiative to preserve such evidence.

### Case[2]

Some day before 15 March 2000, Mr. Zhu and 8 other co-plaintiffs filed a lawsuit against the Hangzhou Jinyuan Hotel in the Shangcheng District People's Court of Hangzhou Municipality. The co-plaintiffs asserted that they had discovered a "red head big fly" in a plate of shrimps during a meal in the Hangzhou Jinyuan Hotel. The co-plaintiffs made

---

[2] See Ye Qing *et al.* (eds.), Minshi susongfa (*Civil Procedure Law*), Law Press China, Beijing 2006, pp. 108-110.

representations to the hotel. In the course of quarrel, Mr. Liu, a manager of the hotel grabbed the rare object and swallowed it. That night the co-plaintiffs requested an extension of apology and sought 50000 yuan RMB in intangible damages from the defendant.

The case was tried on 29 June 2000. The point at issue was whether the above-mentioned rare object had been a "red head big fly". During the court's session, the lawyer of the defendant was approved by the presiding judge and held a serving tray in both hands. 5 living "red head big flies" were put on the serving tray. They were heated up over an alcoholic stove after having been shown to the presiding judge, the co-plaintiffs and the defendant. Being heated up, the 5 "red head big flies" turned totally black; no part of these flied was red. On these grounds, the defendant argued that the dignity of the co-plaintiffs had not been infringed upon, and that the litigation claims of the co-plaintiffs had been groundless in law.

Obviously influenced by this process of proof, the Shangcheng District People's Court rendered a judgement of first instance on 17 October 2000, according to which the rare object in the plate at that night was not a "red head big fly" but an "uncertified flying object". As a result, the defendant was sentenced to compensate the co-plaintiffs 216 yuan RMB in damages. Other litigation claims of the co-plaintiffs were overruled. The litigation costs of 2010 yuan RMB were to be shared by the co-plaintiffs (1510 yuan RMB) and the defendant (500 yuan RMB).

In the instant case, the co-plaintiffs should have undertaken the burden of proof (Article 64 of the CPL). They had to proof that the rare object had been a "red head big fly".

However, the principal evidence of this case had been destroyed by the defendant. The evidence had been under the control of the defendant and was possible to be destroyed by the defendant at anytime. Accordingly, the defendant should proof that the rare object in the plate had not been a "red head big fly".

Evidence should have authenticity, relevancy and lawfulness. The evidence proffered by the defendant's lawyer was not sufficient. As to lawfulness, it didn't belong to any of the categories of evidence listed in Article 65 of the CPL. Finally, it was not the original fly.

# Chapter Six Time Periods and Service

## I. Time Periods

### A. In General (Article 75 of the CPL)

Time periods in the CPL include periods prescribed by the law and periods designated by the court.

They shall be calculated by the hour, the day, the month and the year. The hour and day from which a time period begins shall not be counted.

If the expiration date of a time period falls on a holiday, then the day immediately following the holiday shall be regarded as the expiration date.

A time period shall not include the traveling time.

### B. Application of Extension for Justified Reasons *e.g. Force Majeure*

In case of failure of a party to meet a deadline due to *force majeure* or for other justified reasons, the party concerned may apply for an extension of the time limit within 10 days after the obstacle is removed. The application is subject to approval by a court (Article 76 of the CPL).

#### Case: Xu Ying versus Yang Di

Mr. Yang Di is an Oversee Chinese of American nationality – he resides abroad without domicile in China. His wife Xu Ying is a Chinese citizen.

In March 1998 Xu Ying filed a lawsuit in the people's court of District S in City H, requesting divorce from Yang

Di.

On 23 April 1998Yang Di received a copy of the statement of complaint.

On 8 May 1998Yang Di objected to the jurisdiction of the people's court of District S in City H.

Refusal by the court in form of a written order was served on Yang on 20 May 1998.

Mr. Yang Di signed this and did not appeal right away.

On 18 June 1998 Mr. Yang Di appealed to the next superior court against the written order made by the people's court of District S in City H.

Was the appeal filed in time?

Article 247 of the CPL gives a 30-day period for the right of appeal, starting from the date of service or the date of issuance of the written judgment. Thus the 30-day time period ends on 19 June 1998. The appeal was filed in time.

## Case: Xu versus Real Estate Agent[1]

Xu had the right to use an apartment in Haidian District, Zhichun Road from 8 October 2003 to 7 October 2004. The rent is 1,600 RMB per month. According to the lease contract, the deposit is one monthly rent. After expiration of the contract, within one month, the real estate agent should return the deposit to Xu, after subtracting utilities. If Xu rescinds the contract, he must give notice one month prior. On 7 January 2004, the parties examined the articles in the apartment. Both signed an agreement to terminate the contract and agreed that all obligations towards each other would end.

[1] See Ye Qing *et al.* (eds.), Minshi susongfa (*Civil Procedure Law*), Law Press China, Beijing 2006, pp. 125-128.

But on 27 June 2004, Xu filed a lawsuit in Haidian District People's Court stating the real estate agent had received and not properly returned the deposit. Haidian District People's Court said that Xu's suit did not conform to the formal legal requirements. It required for Xu to amend his suit within two days. On 5 July 2004, Haidian District People's Court accepted the case. A copy of the statement of complaint was served on the defendant on 9 July 2004. The defendant was informed that he should present his arguments within 15 days. Trial commenced in Haidian District People's Court, which rendered a judgment on 20 December 2004, rejecting the plaintiff's argument. Court costs of 74 RMB were to be paid by the plaintiff. On 27 December 2004, the judgment was served on both parties – with both parties being informed of their right of appeal. On 10 January 2005, the plaintiff filed an appeal to the next superior court – the Beijing Municipal No. I Intermediate People's Court. This court accepted the appeal of the plaintiff. It ruled that the application of law by the court of first instance was wrong. The result of the judgment was improper.

On 20 March 2005, the court referred to Article 153 Paragraph 1 Number 2 of the CPL – if the court of first instance rendered a judgment based on an incorrect application of the law, the judgment shall be amended according to the law.

The court nullified the judgment of first instance and the real estate agent was ordered to return the deposit within 10 days. The court costs of first instance had to be borne by the real estate agent. The court of second instance was the final court.

## II. Service

For every litigation document that is served, a receipt bearing the date of receipt noted by the signature or seal of the person on whom the document was served has to be issued. The date of receipt is regarded as the date of service (Article 77 of the CPL).

There are the following methods of service for litigation documents: (1) direct service, *i.e.* litigation documents are sent or delivered directly to the person on whom they are to be served; (2) leaving the litigation documents at the place where the person on whom they are to be served lives (Article 78 of the CPL); (3) service entrusted to another people's court; (4) service by mail (the date stated on the receipt for postal delivery is deemed the date of service, Article 80 of the CPL); (5) service forwarded (to servicemen through the political organ of the unit at or above the regimental level in the army forces (Article 81 of the CPL), on persons in imprisonment through the prison authorities or the unit of reform through labor, on persons undergoing rehabilitation through labor through the unit of rehabilitation through labor (Article 82 of the CPL); (6) service by public announcement – 60 days after the public announcement is made, the documents shall be deemed to have been served (Article 84 of the CPL).

### Case[2]

On 20 September 2003, Bi filed a lawsuit against Li and Zhang. A copy of the statement of complaint was sent to Li

[2] See Ye Qing *et al.* (eds.), Minshi susongfa (*Civil Procedure Law*), Law Press China, Beijing 2006, pp. 129.

and Zhang within 5 days. The trial took place on 16 October 2003. On 3 November 2003, the court requested the parties to appear in court again. On 6 November 2003, Li and Zhang appeared in court but Bi did not. Bi's whereabouts were unknown. The court made service by public announcement. On 9 November 2003, the court drafted a public announcement: "Mr. Bi, the case has been tried and dismissed. You are required to come to the court to take the judgment within 60 days starting from the issuance of this public announcement". This statement had been published in a nationwide newspaper.

# Chapter Seven Property Preservation and Advance Execution

## I. Property Preservation

### A. Preconditions of the Adoption of Measures for Property Preservation (Article 92 of the CPL)

In cases where the execution of a judgment may become impossible or difficult because of the acts of either party or for other reasons, the people's court may, at the application of the other party, order the adoption of measures for property preservation. If no party applies for preservation, the people's court may itself order the adoption of measures for property preservation where necessary.

### B. Application (Article 93 of the CPL)

Any interested party whose lawful rights and interests would, due to urgent circumstances, suffer irretrievable damage without the adoption of measures for property preservation, may apply to the people's court for the adoption such measures. The application has to be made before the filing of a lawsuit concerning the property. The applicant may be enjoined by the people's court to provide security; if he fails to provide security, his application shall be rejected (Article 92 of the CPL).

### C. Limit and Methods of Property Preservation

Property preservation measures shall be limited to the scope of the claims or to the property relevant to the case.

Property preservation shall be set into effect by sealing up, distraining, freezing or other methods as prescribed by the law (Article 94 of the CPL).

### D. Cancellation of Property Preservation Measures

If the person against whom the application for property preservation measures is made provides security, the people's court shall cancel the order for property preservation measures (Article 95 of the CPL).

## II. Advance Execution

### A. Characteristics

The people's court may, upon application of the party concerned, order advance execution in the following cases:

(1) cases involving claims for alimony, support for children or elders, pension for the disabled or the family of a decedent, or expenses for medical care;

(2) cases involving claims for remuneration for labor; and

(3) cases involving urgent circumstances that require advance execution (Article 97 of the CPL).

### B. Conditions of the Cases

Cases in which advance execution is ordered by the people's court shall meet the following conditions:

(1) the relationship of rights and obligations between the parties concerned is clear and definite, and denial of advance execution would seriously affect the livelihood or production operations of the applicant; and

(2) the person against whom the application is made is

capable of fulfilling his obligations (Article 98 Paragraph 1 of the CPL).

### C. Security

The people's court may enjoin the applicant to provide security; if he fails to provide security, his application shall be rejected (Article 98 Paragraph 2 of the CPL).

## III. Reconsideration

If the party concerned is not satisfied with the order for property preservation or execution, he may apply for reconsideration. Execution of the order is not suspended during the time of reconsideration (Article 99 of the CPL).

# Chapter Eight Compulsory Measures against Obstruction of Civil Proceedings

## I. Acts of Obstruction of Civil Proceedings and Compulsory Measures against Them

### A. The Defendant's Refusal to Appear in Court without Justified Reason

If a defendant is required to appear in court, but, having been served twice with summons, still refuses to appear in court without justification, the people's court may constrain the defendant to appear in court by a peremptory writ (Article 100 of the CPL)

### B. Violation of the Court Rules

In general, participants and other persons in the court proceedings have an obligation to abide by the court rules. If a person violates the court rules, the people's court may reprimand him, or order him to leave the courtroom, or impose a fine on him or detain him. A person who seriously disrupts court order by making an uproar in the court or rushing at, insulting, slandering, threatening, or assaulting the adjudication officers, shall be investigated for criminal responsibility by the people's court; if the offence is a minor one, the offender may be detained or a fine may be imposed on him (See Article 101 of the CPL).

## C. Obstruction of the Trial of a Case before the People's Court

If a participant or any other person in the proceedings commits one of the following acts, the people's court shall impose a fine on him or detain him, according to the seriousness of the act; if the act constitutes a crime, the offender shall be investigated for criminal responsibility according to law (with respect to a citizen):

(1) forging or destroying important evidence, obstructing the trial of a case by the court;

(2) using violence, threats or subornation to prevent a witness from giving testimony, or instigating, suborning, or coercing others to commit perjury;

(3) concealing, transferring, selling or destroying property that has been sealed up or distrained, or property of which an inventory has been made and which has been put under his care according to court instruction, or transferring property that has been frozen;

(4) insulting, slandering, incriminating with false charges, assaulting or maliciously retaliating against adjudication officers or personnel, participants in the proceedings, witnesses, interpreters, evaluation experts, inspectors, or personnel assisting in execution;

(5) using violence, threats or other means to hinder adjudication officers or personnel from performing their duties; or

(6) refusing to carry out legally effective judgments or orders of the people's court.

With respect to a unit that commits anyone of the acts specified above, the people's court may impose a fine on it or detain its principal heads or the persons who are to be held actually responsible for the act; if the act constitutes a crime, investigations for criminal responsibility shall be made by the people's court (Article 102 of the CPL).

### D. Acts Committed by a Unit Which Is under an Obligation to Assist in Investigation and Execution

Examples of such acts are as follows (see Article 103 of the CPL): refusing or obstructing the investigation and collection of evidence by the people's court; refusing to provide other obligatory assistance in the execution.

With respect to a citizen, compulsory measures may include: enjoining the unit concerned to perform its obligation, or imposing a fine.

With respect to a unit, compulsory measures may include: a fine on its principal heads or the persons who are to be held actually responsible for the act, or putting forward a judicial proposal to the relevant organ *e.g.* supervisory organ.

## II. Compulsory Measures (Details)

### A. Types of Compulsory Measures Subject to the Approval of the Court President

The following compulsory measures shall be subject to the approval of the president of the people's court (Article 105 of the CPL):

**1. Imposition of a Fine**

A fine on an individual shall not exceed 10000 yuan RMB. A fine on a unit shall not be less than 10000 yuan RMB and shall not exceed 300000 yuan RMB (see Article 104 of the CPL, amended on 28 October 2007, effective as of 1 April 2008).

**2. Imposition of a Detention**

The period of detention shall not be longer than 15 days.

The people's court shall deliver detained persons to a public security organ for custody. The people's court may decide to advance the time of release (see Article 104 of the CPL).

**3. Constrained Appearance in Court**

A peremptory writ shall be issued for constraining appearance in court.

## B. Relevant Decisions

Decision on the adoption of compulsory measures against obstruction of proceedings shall be made by the court (Article 106 of the CPL). For the imposition of a fine or detention, a decision in writing shall be made (see Article 105 of the CPL).

# Chapter Nine Litigation Costs

## I. Main Provision of the CPL on Litigation Costs

Any party filing a civil lawsuit shall pay court costs. In addition to the court costs, the party shall pay other fees for property cases. However, any party that has genuine difficulty in paying litigation costs may apply to the people's court for deferment or reduction of the payment or for its exemption. Particulars for payment of litigation costs shall be laid down separately (Article 107 of the CPL).

The Measures for Payment of Litigation Costs (containing 56 articles) were adopted on 8 December 2006 at the 159th standing meeting of the State Council. They came into effect on 1 April 2007.[1] Any party filing a civil lawsuit or an administrative lawsuit shall pay court costs in accordance with the Measures (Article 2 of the Measures). This also applies to foreigners, stateless persons, foreign enterprises or organizations filing lawsuits in a people's court (Article 5 of the Measures). According to Article 29 of the Measures, litigation costs shall be paid by the losing party, unless they are voluntarily borne by the winning party. If the case is partially won

---

1 See Zhonghua renmin gongheguo zuigao renmin fayuan gongbao (*Gazette of the Supreme People's Court of the PRC*), No. 3/2007, pp. 3-9.

or partially lost by the parties, the people's court shall decide the amount of litigation cost borne by each party. If a party to a joint action loses the case, the people's court shall decide the amount of litigation cost borne by each member of the party based on his interests to the object of action.

# Chapter Ten Ordinary Procedure of First Instance

## I. Bringing a Lawsuit and Entertaining a Case

### A. Conditions of Bringing a Lawsuit

The following conditions must be met when a lawsuit is brought (Article 108 of the CPL):

(1) the plaintiff must be a citizen, legal person or any other organization having a direct interest;

(2) there must be a definite defendant;

(3) there must be a specific claim or specific claims, facts and causes for the suit; and

(4) the suit must be within the scope of acceptance for civil actions by the people's courts and under the jurisdiction of the entertaining people's court.

### B. Statement of Complaint

When a lawsuit is brought, a statement of complaint shall be submitted to the people's court, copies of the statement of complaint shall be provided according to the number of defendants.

The statement of complaint is normally presented in writing, but the complaint may be stated orally in exceptional cases (Article 109 of the CPL).

### C. Time Limit of Acceptance and Rejection

The court shall place the case on the docket within 7 days if the statement of complaint meets the requirements for acceptance. If the statement of complaint does not meet the requirements for acceptance, the court shall make an order to reject it within 7 days (Article 112 of the CPL).

## II. Preparation for Trial

### A. Time Limit for Filing a Defense

The people's court shall send a copy of the statement of complaint to the defendant within 5 days after docketing the case. The defendant shall file a defense within 15 days from the receipt of the copy of the statement of complaint.

When the defendant files a defense, the people's court shall send a copy of the statement of defense to the plaintiff within 5 days from its receipt (Article 113 of the CPL).

### B. Investigations

The adjudication officers must carry out investigations and collect the necessary evidence. If needed, a people's court may entrust a people's court in another locality with the investigations (Articles 116-118 of the CPL).

## III. Trial in Court

### A. Public Trial

In principle, civil cases shall be tried publicly, except for cases involving State secrets or personal privacy; divorce cases or cases involving trade secrets may not be tried publicly if so requested by one party (Article 120 of the CPL).

### B. Court Session

The people's court shall notify the participants in the proceedings 3 days before the opening of a court session (Article 122 of the CPL).

Before the court session is called to order, the court clerk shall ascertain whether or not the parties and other participants in the proceedings are present and announce the rules of order of the court (Article 123 Paragraph 1 of the CPL).

At the beginning of a court session, the presiding judge shall check whether the parties are present, announce the cause of action and the names of the adjudication officers and court clerks, inform the parties of the relevant litigation rights and obligations, and ask the parties whether or not they wish to apply for the withdrawal of any court personnel (Article 123 Paragraph 1 of the CPL).

### C. Court Investigation

Court investigation shall be conducted in the following order (Article 124 of the CPL):

(1) statements by the parties;

(2) informing the witnesses of their rights and obligations, having the witnesses give testimony and reading the written statements of absent witnesses;

(3) presentation of evidence (the parties may present new evidence during a court session, see Article 125 of the CPL);

(4) reading of expert conclusions;

(5) reading of records of inspection.

### D. Trial in Combination

Additional claims by the plaintiff, counterclaims by the defendant and third-party claims related to the case may be tried in combination (Article 126 of the CPL).

### E. Court Debate

The debate shall be conducted in the following order (Article 127 of the CPL):

(1) oral statements by the plaintiff and his agents *ad litem*;

(2) defense by the defendant and his agents *ad litem*;

(3) oral statement or defense by the third party and his agents *ad litem*;

(4) debate between the two sides;

(5) final opinion of the plaintiff, the defendant and the third party.

### F. Judgment

A judgment shall be rendered if mediation efforts fail (Article 128 of the CPL).

A judgment by default may be made under certain conditions (Articles 129-131 of the CPL).

The people's court shall publicly pronounce its judgment in all cases, whether publicly tried or not (Article 134 of the CPL).

Upon pronouncement of a judgment, the parties concerned must be informed of their right to file an appeal, the time limit for appeal and the appellate court.

Upon pronouncement of a divorce judgment, the parties concerned must be informed not to remarry before the judgment takes effect.

# IV. Suspension and Termination of Legal Proceedings

## A. Suspension of Legal Proceedings

**1. Causes of the suspension of legal proceedings are as follows (Article 136 of the CPL):**

(1) one of the parties dies and it is necessary to wait for the heir or heiress to make clear whether he or she wants to participate in the proceedings or not;

(2) one of the parties loses its capacity to engage in litigation and his agent *ad litem* has not yet been designated;

(3) the legal person or any other organization, being one of the parties, is dissolved, and the successor to its rights and obligations has not yet been determined;

(4) one of the parties is unable to participate in the proceedings for reasons of *force majeure*;

(5) the adjudication of the case pending is dependent on the results of the trial of another case that has not yet been concluded; or

(6) other circumstances have occurred that warrant the suspension to the litigation.

**2. Resumption of the Proceedings**

The proceedings shall resume after the causes of the suspension have been eliminated.

## B. Termination of Legal Proceedings

Legal proceedings shall be terminated in any of the following circumstances (Article 137 of the CPL):

(1) the plaintiff dies without a successor, or the successor waives the right to litigate;

(2) the defendant dies leaving no estate, nor anyone to fulfill his obligations;

(3) one of the parties in a divorce case dies; or

(4) one of the parties dies being a claimant to alimony, support for elders or children or the party being a claimant to the termination of an adoptive relationship.

## V. Judgment and Order

### A. Judgment

A judgment shall clearly set forth the following contents (Article 138 Paragraph 1 of the CPL):

(1) cause of action, the claims, facts and cause or causes of the dispute;

(2) the facts and causes as found in the judgment and the basis of application of law;

(3) the outcome of adjudication and the costs to be borne;

(4) the time limit for filing an appeal and the appellate court.

The judgment shall be signed by the adjudication officers and the court clerk, with the seal of the court (Article 138 Paragraph 2 of the CPL).

A judgment on one part of the case may be passed first if some of the facts in a case are already evident (Article 139 of the CPL).

### B. Written Order

An order in writing is to be made in any of the following conditions (Article 140 of the CPL):

(1) refusal to entertain a case (subject to appeal);

(2) reply to an objection to the jurisdiction of a court (subject to appeal);

(3) rejection of a complaint (subject to appeal);

(4) property preservation and advance execution;

(5) approval or disapproval of withdrawal of a suit;

(6) suspension or termination of legal proceedings;

(7) correction of errata in the judgment;

(8) suspension or termination of execution;

(9) refusal to enforce an arbitration award;

(10) refusal to enforce a document of a notary office evidencing the rights of a creditor and entitling him to its compulsory execution;

(11) other matters not to be dealt with by judgment.

## C. Finality of Judgments and Written Orders

All judgments and written orders of the Supreme People's Court, judgments and written orders that may not be appealed according to the law, judgments and written orders that have not been appealed within the prescribed time limit shall be legally effective (Article 141 of the CPL).

# Chapter Eleven Summary Procedure

## I. Scope of Application

The summary procedure applies to the trial of simple civil cases in which the facts are evident, the rights and obligations clear and the disputes trivial in character. It is applied by the basic people's courts and the tribunals dispatched by them (Article 142 of the CPL).

## II. Parties in a Summary Procedure

In simple civil cases, the plaintiff may file his complaint orally. The two parties may at the same time come before a basic people's court or a tribunal dispatched by it for a solution of their dispute (Article 143 of the CPL, Paragraph 1 and Paragraph 2 Sentence 1).

## III. Other Features

The basic people's court or the tribunal dispatched by it may try the simple civil case immediately or set a date for the trial (Article 143 of the CPL, Paragraph 2 Sentence 2). It may use simplified methods to summon at any time the parties and witnesses (Article 144 of the CPL).

Simple civil cases shall be tried by a single judge alone (Article 145 of the CPL). The people's court trying a case in which summary procedure is followed shall conclude the case within 3 months after being placed on the docket (Article 146 of the CPL).

## Case

Villager Jia and villager Liu had a dispute over trivial civil matters. During the quarrel Liu unintentionally wounded Jia. Jia took Liu immediately to the dispatched tribunal of the county people's court in the township and instituted a civil lawsuit against Liu requesting compensation. Adjudicative assessor Zheng heard the statement of complaint by Jia and questioned Liu in a simple manner. A judgment was rendered by adjudicative assessor Zheng immediately with the seal of the dispatched tribunal in the township.

Was this lawful?

Answer: Firstly, Zheng was not a judge, therefore, he could not try the case alone. Secondly, the seal of the county people's court and not the seal of its dispatched tribunal in the township should haven been put on the judgment.

# Chapter Twelve Procedure of Second Instance

## I. Conditions and Time Limits for an Appeal

### A. Appeal against a Judgment

If a party refuses to accept a judgment of first instance of a local people's court, he shall have the right to file an appeal with the people's court at the next higher level within 15 days after the date of service of the written judgment (Article 147 Paragraph 1 of the CPL).

### B. Appeal against a Written Order

If a party refuses to accept a written order of first instance of a local people's court, he shall have the right to file an appeal with the people's court at the next higher level within 10 days after the date of service of the written order (Article 147 Paragraph 2 of the CPL).

## II. Appeal Petition

For filing an appeal, a petition for the purpose of appeal shall be submitted.

### A. Content of the Appeal Petition

The content of the appeal petition shall include the names of the parties, the name of the people's court where the case was originally tried, the file number of the case, the cause of action, and the claims of and the reasons for the appeal (Article 148 of the CPL).

### B. Submission

The appeal petition shall be submitted through the people's court which originally tried the case. If a party appeals directly to a people's court of second instance, the said court shall within 5 days transmit the appeal petition to the people's court which originally tried the case (Article 149 of the CPL).

## III. Defense

The people's court which originally tried the case shall serve a copy of the appeal petition on the other party within 5 days after receiving the appeal petition. The other party shall submit his defense within 15 days from the receipt of the copy. The people's court shall, within 5 days after receiving the defense, serve a copy of the defense on the appellant (Article 150 Paragraph 1 of the CPL).

## IV. Several Aspects of the Second Instance

### A. Beginning

After receiving the appeal petition and the defense, the people's court which originally tried the case shall deliver them together with the entire case file and evidence to the people's court of second instance (Article 150 Paragraph 2 of the CPL).

### B. Nature of the Second Instance

The court of second instance shall review the relevant facts and the application of law (Article 151 of the CPL).

### C. Collegial Panel

A collegial panel shall be formed to conduct the trial. If the panel, after having verified the facts of the case through consultation of the files, investigations and questionings of the parties, considers it unnecessary to conduct a trial, it may render a judgment or a written order immediately (Article 152 Paragraph 1 of the CPL).

## V. Outcomes of the Procedure of Second Instance

After trying a case on appeal, there will be one of the following outcomes (Article 153 of the CPL):

(1) The appeal is rejected in the form of a judgment and the original judgment is affirmed if the facts were clearly ascertained and the law was correctly applied in the original judgment.

(2) The original judgment is amended according to the law if the application of the law was incorrect in the original judgment.

(3) The court of second instance makes a written order to set aside the original judgment and remand the case to the original court for retrial (which may be subject to appeal), or the court of second instance may amend the judgment after investigating and clarifying the facts if in the original judgment the facts were incorrectly or not clearly ascertained and the evidence was insufficient.

(4) The judgment is set aside by a written order and the case is remanded to the original court for retrial (which may be subject to appeal) if there was violence of legal procedure

in making the original judgment, which may have affected correct adjudication.

## VI. Mediation in a Case on Appeal

Mediation may be conducted by a people's court of second instance. With the service of the mediation statement, the original judgment of the lower court is deemed as set aside (Article 155 of the CPL).

## VII. Finality and Periods

The judgment and the written order of a people's court of second instance shall be final (Article 158 of the CPL).

Normally, a case of appeal shall be concluded within 3 months after docketing the case. Extension of the period is subject to the approval of the president of the appellate court. In a case on appeal against a written order, a final written order shall be made by the appellate court within 30 days (Article 159 of the CPL).

### Case

The parties were Mr. Ding and Mr. Shi. Mr. Shi signed a contract of lease on 13 March 2004 for an apartment. According to the contract, the time limit for rent was 1 year. Mr. Shi is the owner of the apartment. Mr. Ding said that he needed to use the apartment urgently, and he would arrange the repairs to the apartment. Mr. Ding said if any problems arise, he (Mr. Ding) would have to bear the responsibility.

On 29 July 2004, one brick fell from the roof of the apartment and hit Mr. Ding. The plaintiff Mr. Ding filed a lawsuit in the District People's Court of Shangrao Municipality, Jiangxi Province on 18 August 2004, requesting the defendant Mr. Shi to pay for his medical treatment and other losses due to the absence from work, in total 18692 yuan RMB.

The court of first instance rendered a judgment against the defendant, supporting the plaintiff's complaint. The defendant Mr. Shi filed an appeal within 2 days in the Shangrao Municipality Intermediate People's Court, Jiangxi Province.

During the appeal, the appellant Mr. Shi provided new evidence showing that he had reached an agreement with the plaintiff Mr. Ding on 23 April 2004 according to which any damages caused by the defects of the apartment were to be borne by Mr. Ding. The court of second instance held that the facts had been ascertained clearly, and the application of law had been appropriate. A sole judge tried the appeal. During the trial it was discovered that the plaintiff Mr. Ding had owed the appellant Mr. Shi rent in the sum of 2000 yuan RMB which had not yet been paid. In order to try the case efficiently, the court of second instance tried the two cases combined. As a result, the appellant Mr. Shi was ordered to pay 18692−2000 yuan RMB, all together 16692 yuan RMB.

# Chapter Thirteen  Special Procedure

## I. Types of Cases

Four types of cases are subject to the provisions concerning special procedure of the CPL (Chapter XV, Articles 160-176 of the CPL):

(1) cases concerning the qualification of voters;

(2) cases concerning the declaration of a person as missing or dead;

(3) cases concerning the assessment of legal incapacity or restricted legal capacity of citizens;

(4) cases concerning the determination of property as ownerless.

## II. Characteristics

### A. Finality of the Judgment

The judgment of first instance of cases tried in accordance with the special procedure shall be final (see Article 161 of the CPL).

### B. Single Judge

Cases in which special procedure is followed shall be tried in principle by a single judge alone. Nevertheless, for the trial of cases involving the qualification of voters or of major, difficult or complicated cases, a collegial panel of judges shall be formed (see Article 161 of the CPL).

## C. Time limit

Cases in which special procedure is followed shall be concluded within 30 days after placing the case on the docket by the court, or within 30 days after expiration of the period stated in the public notice. Any extension of the time limit is subject to the approval of the president of the court, except for cases concerning the qualification of voters (Article 163 of the CPL).

# Chapter Fourteen  Procedure of Trial Supervision

## I. Conditions for a Retrial

### A. Definite Error in a Legally Effective Judgment or Written Order

If the president of a people's court at any level finds definite error in a legally effective judgment or written order of his court and deems it necessary to have the case retried, he shall refer it to the adjudication committee for discussion and decision (Article 177 of the CPL). If the Supreme People's Court finds definite error in a legally effective judgment or written order of a local people's court at any level, or if a people's court at a higher level finds some definite errors in a legally effective judgment or written order of a people's court at a lower level, it shall respectively have the power to bring the case up for trial by itself or direct the people's court at a lower level to conduct a retrial (Article 177 of the CPL).

### B. Decision Makers

The president of a people's court, the Supreme People's Court or a people's court at a higher level shall make the decision as to a retrial.

### C. Application Made by a Party to an Action

If a party to an action considers that there is error in a legally effective judgment or written order, he may apply to a people's court at the next higher level for a retrial; however, the execution of the judgment or the order shall not be suspended (Article 178 of the CPL, amended on 28 October 2007, effective as of 1 April 2008).

Other preconditions to the application made by a party are (see Article 179 of the CPL):

(1) there is sufficient new evidence to set aside the original judgment or written order;

(2) the facts which were ascertained in the original judgment or written order lack evidence to prove them;

(3) the main evidence for the facts ascertained in the original judgment or written order was falsified;

(4) the main evidence for the facts ascertained in the original judgment or written order has not been cross-examined;

(5) any party to a lawsuit was unable to collect the evidence necessary for adjudicating the case due to objective reasons and had applied, in writing, to the people's court for investigation and collection of such evidence, but the people's court has failed to investigate and collect the evidence;

(6) there has been a definite error in the application of law in the original judgment or written order;

(7) in violation of legal provisions, the jurisdiction was erroneously exercised;

(8) the formation of the adjudicative organization was unlawful or the adjudicative personnel that should have withdrawn failed to do so;

(9) a person having no capacity to engage in litigation has not been represented by a statutory agent, or the party that should have participated in the litigation failed to do so for reasons not attributable to himself or his agent *ad litem*;

(10) in violation of legal provisions, a party's right to

debate was deprived of;

(11) a default judgment in the absence of a party was rendered whereas that party had not been served with summons;

(12) claims have been omitted exceeded in the original judgment or written order; or

(13) the legal document on which the original judgment or written order was based has been abrogated or revised.

As to the situations where there was violation of the statutory procedure which may have affected the correctness of the judgment or written order, or the adjudication officers have committed, while adjudicating the case, acts of embezzlement, bribes, malpractice for personal benefits and acts of perverting the law in the adjudication, the people's courts shall retry the case.

If a party applies for a retrial, he shall submit a written application for retrial and other materials. The people's court shall, within 5 days after receiving the application, serve the duplicate of the written application for retrial on the other party. The other party shall submit written opinions within 15 days after receiving the said duplicate; and failure on the part of the other party to submit the written opinions shall not prevent the review by the people's court (Article 180 of the CPL).

The people's court shall complete the review of the written application for retrial within 3 months after receiving it, and shall rule to retry the case if the application meets the conditions specified in one of the subparagraphs of Article 179 of the CPL; otherwise, it shall rule to reject the application. Under special circumstances where the period of time for review needs to be extended, the matter shall be subject to approval by the president of the court (Article 181 Paragraph 1 of the CPL). If a case is ruled to be retried upon application by a party to the action, the case shall be retried by an intermediate people's court or a people's court at a higher level. If a case is ruled to be retied by the Supreme People's Court or a high peoples court, the case shall be retried by the court that rules in favor of retrial or it may be handed over to any other people's court or the people's court that originally tried the case for retrial (Paragraph 2 of Article 181 of the CPL).

With respect to a legally effective mediation statement, if evidence furnished by a party proves that the mediation has violated the principle of voluntariness, or that the content of the mediation statement has violated the law, the party may apply for a retrial. If the forgoing has been examined by the people's court as being true, a retrial shall be conducted (Article 182 of the CPL).

With respect to a legally effective judgment on the dissolution of a marriage, no party may apply for a retrial (Article 183 of the CPL).

The application for a retrial has to be made by a party within 2 years after the judgment or written order becomes legally effective (Article 184 of the CPL).

## II. Procedure of Trial Supervision

### A. Procedures of Retrial

With respect to a case pending retrial by a people's court in accordance with the procedure for retrial supervision, the case shall be tried in accordance with the procedure of first instance, and the new judgment or order may be appealed, if the legally effective judgment or written order was made by a court of first instance. If the legally effective judgment or written order was made by a court of second instance, the case shall be tried in accordance with the procedure of second instance, and the new judgment or order shall be legally effective. If it is a case which was brought up for trial by a court at a higher level, it shall be tried in accordance with the procedure of second instance, and the new judgment or written order shall be legally effective (Article 186 Paragraph 1 of the CPL).

### B. New Collegial Panel

The people's court shall form a new collegial panel for the purpose of the retrial (Paragraph 2 of Article 186 of the CPL).

## III. Protest Lodged by the Supreme People's Procuratorate or a People's Procuratorate at a Higher Level in accordance with the Procedure of Trial Supervision

### A. Conditions

If the Supreme People's Procuratorate finds that a legally effective judgment or written order made by a people's court at any level involves any of the circumstances prescribed by Article 179 Paragraph 1 of the CPL, or if a people's procuratorate at a higher level finds that a legally effective judgment or written order made by a people's court at a lower level involves any of the circumstances prescribed by Article 179 Paragraph 1 of the CPL, the Supreme People's

Procuratorate or the people's procuratorate at a higher level shall respectively lodge a protest in accordance with the procedure of trial supervision (see Article 187 Paragraph 1 of the CPL).

If a local people's procuratorate at any level finds that a legally effective judgment or written order made by a people's court at the corresponding level involves any of the circumstances specified by Article 179 Paragraph 1 of the CPL, it shall refer the matter to the people's procuratorate at a higher level requesting a protest to be lodged in accordance with the procedure of trial supervision (see Article 187 Paragraph 2 of the CPL).

### B. Protest Made by the People's Procuratorate

With respect to cases in which a protest was filed by a people's procuratorate, the people's court that accepts the protest shall, within 30 days after receiving the protest in writing, make a written order for retrial; if any of the circumstances prescribed by Items 1 to 5 of Article 179 Paragraph 1 of the CPL are involved, it may transfer the case to a court at the next lower level to be retried (Article 188 of the CPL).

When deciding to lodge a protest, the people's procuratorate shall make the protest in writing (Article 189 of the CPL).

The people's court shall, in retrying a case in which protest was lodged by a people's procuratorate, notify the procuratorate to send representative to attend the court session (Article 190 of the CPL).

# Chapter Fifteen Procedure of Execution

## I. General Principles

### A. Legal Documents to be Executed

Legal documents which are to be executed are (see Article 201 Paragraph 1 of the CPL): legally effective judgments or written orders in civil cases (type A), parts of judgments or written orders relating to property in criminal cases (type B), and other legal documents (type C).

### B. Executing Court

For legal documents of type A or C, the executing court is the people's court of first instance; for legal documents of type B, the executing court is the people's court of the locality of the property (Article 207 Paragraph 2 of the CPL).

### C. Execution Officer

The function of the execution officer is to carry out the execution work. He has the duty to produce his credentials when carrying out a compulsory execution measure, to take records of the particulars of the execution, and to have it signed or sealed (Article 209 of the CPL).

### D. Entrustment of Execution

If a person or property subjected to execution is in another locality, the people's court in that locality may be entrusted with the carrying out of the execution. The entrusted people's court shall begin the execution within 15 days after receiving the letter of entrustment (Article 210 of the CPL).

# II. Application for Execution and Referral

## A. Application for Execution

Preconditions for application for execution may be:

(1) a party has refused to comply with legally effective judgments or written orders;

(2) a party has refused to comply with the mediation statement and other legal documents that are to be executed by the people's court (see Article 216 of the CPL);

(3) a party has failed to comply with an award of an arbitral organ (Article 217 of the CPL); or

(4) a party has failed to comply with a document evidencing the creditor's rights made enforceable by a notary office (Article 218 of the CPL).

## B. Judge's Referral to the Execution Officer for Enforcement

If a party refuses to comply with legally effective judgments or written orders in civil cases, the judge may refer the matter to the execution officer for enforcement (Article 216 Sentence 2 of the CPL).

## C. Time Limit for the Submission of an Application for Execution

Time limit for the submission of an application for execution shall be 1 year, if both or one of the parties are citizens; it shall be 6 months, if both parties are legal persons or other organizations (Article 219 of the CPL).

## III. Execution Measures

Execution measures are (see Articles 221-223 of the CPL):

(1) freezing or transfer of deposits;

(2) withholding or withdrawing part of the income;

(3) sealing up, distraining, freezing, selling by public auction or selling off part of the property; or

(4) issuing a search warrant.

# Part II The Conflict of Laws

# Chapter Sixteen International Jurisdiction under the Chinese International Civil Procedure Law

## I. General Principles of Civil Procedure of Cases Involving Foreign Elements

### A. Special Provisions for Civil Procedure of Cases Involving Foreign Elements

Civil proceedings within the territory of the PRC in regard to cases involving foreign elements are in principle subject to the special provisions of Part Four of the CPL (Articles 235-267).

### B. Priority of International Treaties

If an international treaty concluded or acceded to by the PRC contains provisions that differ from provisions of the CPL, the provisions of the international treaty shall be applied, except those on which China has made reservations (Article 236 of the CPL).

### C. Only Chinese Lawyers Appointed

When foreign nationals, stateless persons or foreign enterprises and organizations need lawyers as agents *ad litem* to bring an action or enter appearance on their behalf in a people's court, they must appoint lawyers of the Peoples Republic of China (Article 239 of the CPL).

### D. Service and Time Periods

A people's court may serve litigation documents on a party who has no domicile within the territory of the PRC in the following ways (Article 245 of the CPL):

(1) in the way specified in international treaties;

(2) service through diplomatic channels;

(3) service entrusted to the Chinese embassy or consulate accredited to the country of residence of the person on whom the service is to be made;

(4) service on the agent *ad litem* who is authorized to receive the documents served;

(5) service on the representative office established in China by the person on whom the service is to be made or on his branch office or business agents having the right to receive the documents;

(6) service by mail; and

(7) service by public notice – the service is deemed completed 6 months from the date on which the public notice was issued.

## II. International Jurisdiction in Civil Matters

A. Contractual Disputes or other Disputes over Property Rights and Interests

With regard to a lawsuit concerning contractual disputes or other disputes over property rights and interests, filed against a defendant who has no domicile within the territory of the PRC,

(1) if the contract is signed or performed within the territory of the PRC, or

(2) if the object of action is located within the territory of the PRC, or

(3) if the defendant has distrainable property within the territory of the PRC , or

(4) if the defendant has its representative office within the territory of the PRC,

the Chinese people's court that has one of the following cases shall have international jurisdiction (Article 241 of the CPL):

a) the people's court at the place where the contract was signed, or

b) the people's court at the place where the contract was performed, or

c) the people's court of the locality of the object of action, or

d) the people's court of the locality of the defendant's distrainable property, or

e) the people's court at the place where the tortious act was committed, or

f) the people's court of the locality of the defendant's representative office.

## B. Choice of Forum

Parties to a dispute over a contract involving foreign elements or over property rights and interests involving foreign elements may, through written agreement, choose the court of the place which has a practical connection with the dispute to exercise international jurisdiction.

If a Chinese people's court is chosen, the provisions of the CPL on jurisdiction by forum level and on exclusive jurisdiction shall not be violated (Article 242 of the CPL).

## C. Tacit Acceptance of the Jurisdiction of a People's Court

If in a civil action in respect of a case involving foreign elements, the defendant raises no objection to the jurisdiction of a people's court and responds to the action by making his defense, he shall be deemed to have accepted that this people's court has jurisdiction over the case (Article 243 of the CPL).

# Chapter Seventeen　Recognition and Enforcement of Foreign Judgments in China

## I. Competent Courts for Applications or Requests of Recognition and Enforcement of Foreign Judgments or Written Orders

If a legally effective judgment or written order made by a foreign court requires recognition and enforcement by a people's court, the party concerned may directly apply for recognition and enforcement to the intermediate people's court which has jurisdiction. The foreign court may also, in accordance with the provisions of the international treaties concluded or acceded to by that foreign country and the PRC or with the principle of reciprocity, request recognition and enforcement by a people's court (Article 265 of the CPL).

## II. Procedure for Recognition and Enforcement of Foreign Judgments or Written Orders in China

In the case of an application or a request for recognition and enforcement of a legally effective judgment or written order of a foreign court, the people's court shall, after examining it in accordance with the international treaties concluded or acceded to by the PRC, or with the principle of reciprocity, and arriving at the conclusion that it does not contradict the primary principles of the law of the PRC nor violates State sovereignty, security and social and public interest of the country, recognize the validity of the judgment or written order, and, if required, issue a writ of execution to enforce it in accordance with the relevant provision of the CPL (Sentence 1 of Article 266 of the CPL).

## III. Refusal of Recognition and Enforcement of Foreign Judgments or Written Orders in the PRC

If the application or request for recognition and enforcement of a legally effective judgment contradicts the primary principles of the law of the PRC or violates State sovereignty, security and social and public interest of the country, the people's court shall not recognize and enforce it (Sentence 1 of Article 266 of the CPL).

# Chapter Eighteen Chinese Choice of Law Rules

## I. Chinese Private International Law (the Law of the Conflict of Laws): Notion

In China as well as abroad, many scholars have defined private international law in different way.

The definition of Cheshire and North is as follows: private international law is that part of English law which comes into operation whenever the court is faced with a claim that contains a foreign element. It is only when this element is present that private international law has function to perform.[1]

The present author has given a definition of private international law as follows: private international law of a country is that part of the legal system of that country, which, when faced with civil and commercial cases involving foreign elements, determines which legal system shall be applicable to civil and commercial legal relationships involving foreign elements, if the countries involved have different substantive private laws in place.[2]

The American Law Institute's Restatement of the Conflict of Laws, Second, adopts as its basic criterion for choice of law the application of the law of the State which has the

---

1 See *Cheshire and North's Private International Law*, Thirteenth Edition (by Peter North and J.J. Fawcett), 1999, p. 3.

2 See Chen Weizuo, Bijiao guoji sifa (*Comparative Private International Law*), Tsinghua University Press, Beijing 2008, pp. 8-9, 46.

most significant relationship to the particular issue under its Paragraph 6. This requires the American court to following a statutory directive of its own State on choice of law but, in the absence of such a directive, the factors relevant to the choice of the applicable law include:

(a) the needs of the interstate and international systems;

(b) the relevant policies of the forum;

(c) the relevant policies of other interested States and the relative interests of those States in the determination of the particular issue;

(d) the protection of justified expectations;

(e) the basic policies underlying the particular field of law;

(f) certainty, predictability and uniformity of result; and

(g) ease in the determination and application of the law to be applied.

The most significant relationship test, with these choice influencing factors, is applied to a whole variety of conflicts issues, ranging from contract and tort to marriage and property.[3]

## Case

Two Businessmen of different nationalities concluded a contract of sale, on the passing of ownership of a movable property to be delivered in Beijing. The seller is of Japanese nationality, the buyer is of Korean nationality. Both have their principal business places in Beijing. A dispute arose between the two people. The seller brought a lawsuit against the buyer

[3] See *Cheshire and North's Private International Law*, Thirteenth Edition (by Peter North and J.J. Fawcett), 1999, pp. 28-29.

in a people's court in a district of Beijing.

Question: which legal system shall govern the contract?

Step 1: Characterization or qualification of the cause of action: contract of sale of internationality.

Step 2: International jurisdiction: do Chinese courts have international jurisdiction over the litigation?

Step 3: Are there rules within the Chinese legal system which claim direct application to the case involving foreign elements? For example, does the CISG (United Nations Convention on Contracts for the International Sale of Goods, adopted at Vienna on 11 April 1980) have to be considered?

Step 4: Which Chinese conflict of laws rule is applicable? Article 126 I of the Contract Law of the PRC of 1999 and Article 145 of the General Principles of Civil Law of the PRC of 1986 may be considered.

Step 5: The determination of the rights and duties (obligations) of the two parties to the contract of sale.

Step 6: The question of recognition and enforcement of the judgement rendered by the Chinese court.

## Case

A man and a woman of Chinese nationality registered their marriage in a civil status authority in Germany. The marriage celebrated in Germany satisfied the formal validity requirements of German law, as well as the essential validity requirements of Chinese law which was their common national law. The couple returned to China. The man filed a lawsuit in the people's court in Beijing against the woman and requested the nullification of the marriage, which had not been registered by a Chinese registrar of civil affairs. The woman wanted to maintain the marriage, while it had satisfied the formal validity requirements of the country of the place of celebration, as well as the essential validity requirements of the national law.

Question: in accordance with which legal system shall the Chinese court render its judgement?

Step 1: Characterization or qualification of the cause of action.

Step 2: International jurisdiction: do Chinese courts have international jurisdiction over the litigation?

Step 3: Are there rules within the Chinese legal system which claim direct application to the case involving foreign elements? For example, do international treaties have to be considered?

Step 4: Which Chinese conflict of laws rule is applicable? Article 188 of the Opinions on the application of the General Principles of Civil Law of the PRC: the *lex loci celebrationis* is applicable when deciding the validity of the marriage celebrated abroad.

Step 5: The determination of the rights and duties (obligations) of the two parties.

Step 6: The question of recognition and enforcement.

## Case

A Chinese woman married a Frenchman in Beijing. They had a daughter, who was cared for by her maternal grandparents in Beijing. Both husband and wife went to France and settled there permanently. The daughter was left in China under the guardianship of her grandparents of the mother side. Husband and wife were divorced in France and were both unwilling to pay maintenance to their daughter. The grandparents instituted a lawsuit against the parents of the child in a people's court in Beijing, requesting the maintenance fees for the child.

Question: which legal system shall be applicable?

Step 1: Characterization or qualification of the cause of action.

Step 2: International jurisdiction: do Chinese courts have international jurisdiction over the litigation?

Step 3: Are there any rules within the Chinese legal system which claim direct application to the case? For example, do international treaties have to be considered?

Step 4: Which Chinese conflict of laws rule is applicable? Article 148 of the General Principles of Civil Law of the PRC: maintenance is governed by the law of the country with which the person to be maintained has the closest connection.

Step 5: The determination of the rights and duties (obligations) of the two parties.

Step 6: The question of recognition and enforcement.

## II. Historical Development of Chinese Private International Law: Towards Codification of China's Private International Law[4]

### A. Introductory Remarks

The PRC has adopted its first systematic and comprehensive statute on private international law since its founding

[4] The content of this section has been published in CHEN Weizuo, *The Necessity of Codification of China's Private International Law and Arguments for a Statute on the Application of Laws as the Legislative Model*, in Tsinghua China Law Review, Vol. 1, No. 1/2009, pp. 1-20.

on 1 October 1949. The Chinese private international law codification process could have been inspired by the historical tradition and past experiences of Chinese legislation on private international law. In order to better understand the current Chinese private international law, it seems useful to have a short survey of Chinese private international law in the light of its historical development, for "the life of the law has not been logic: it has been experience... In order to know what it is, we must know what it has been, and what it tends to become." (Oliver Wendell Holmes, Jr.)[5]

## B. A General Survey of the Necessity of Codification of China's private international law in the Light of Historical Development

### 1. China's Private International Law before 1949

Private international law as a separate branch of law did not previously exist in the long history of traditional Chinese law. One may say that there was no private international law in traditional Chinese law. The notion of private international law (*guoji sifa*) did not exist until it was introduced by scholars during the Qing Dynasty (1644-1911, the last dynasty of imperial China) by translating conflicts works of Japanese scholars into the Chinese language. Accordingly, Chinese legislation on private international law has a history of being inspired by foreign legislative sources.

---

[5] See Oliver Wendell Holmes, Jr., *The Common Law* 5 (1881), cited by Karrer & Arnold, *Switzerland's Private International Law Statute 1987*, p. 1 (Kluwer Law and Taxation Publishers, Deventer 1989); See also *Britannica Online Encyclopedia, Oliver Wendell Holmes, Jr.*, available at http://www.britannica.com/EBchecked/topic/269514/Oliver-Wendell-Holmes-Jr (last visit: 3 April 2011).

In Chinese legal history, the first private international law codification in the modern sense was the Statute on the Application of Laws promulgated by the Peking Government under the Northern Warlords in 1918. The Statute was greatly influenced by the 1898 Japanese Act on the Application of Laws, named *Horei*, and by the 1896 Introductory Act to the German Civil Code (*Einführungsgesetz zum Bürgerlichen Gesetzbuch*, EGBGB), hence it treated nationality as the principal connecting factor in determining the applicable law to various legal relationships. After the coming into power of the Nationalist Party (*Guomindang*) in 1927, the 1918 Statute stayed in force in the mainland of China until the end of the Chinese Civil War in 1949. After 1949, it was merely in force on the Island of Taiwan.

In 1953, a new act named the Law on the Application of Laws to Civil Matters Involving Foreign Elements was promulgated and entered into effect in Taiwan. It remains in force in Taiwan until today[6], having been reformed and modernized on 26 May 2010. Its latest modifications entered into effect on 26 May 2011. Like the old Statute of 1918, the Taiwanese new Law of 1953 follows predominantly the principle of nationality in determining the applicable law, having been influenced by the Japanese *Horei* of 1898 as well as the Introductory Act to the German Civil Code (EGBGB) of 1896.

**2. China's Private International Law in the First Three Decades of the PRC between 1949 and 1979**

The PRC has followed another path of development in its 62 years of legislative history up until the present. In the

[6] See Herbert Han-Pao Ma, *Private International Law of the Republic of China: Past, Present and the Future*, in *Private Law in the International Arena – Liber Amicorum Kurt Siehr*, T.M.C. Asser Press, 2000, pp. 413-428.

first nearly three decades between 1949 and 1978, the Chinese legal system was predominantly influenced by Soviet legal science and ideology. Private international law was greatly ignored and even denied because choice-of-law rules, especially bilateral or multilateral choice-of-law rules which designated not only domestic legal systems but also foreign legal systems as applicable, could lead to the application of foreign laws and even laws of countries of the capitalist world. Neither have systematic statutory choice-of-law rules been enacted, nor has obvious progress been made in private international law during this period, due to the fact that China was fairly isolated during the Cold War and its legislation was greatly influenced by politics and ideology.

**3. China's Private International Law from 1979 until Today**

a. Statutory Conflict Rules

With the end of the so-called Cultural Revolution (1966-1976), Chinese legislation entered a new epoch. In December 1978, the policy of reform and opening to the outside world was officially launched in China. From then on, great changes have taken place in this Asian country, which is the most populated in the world. This is also reflected in a spectacular increase of choice-of-law rules contained in Chinese statutes and regulations.

One of the first statutes containing choice-of-law rules is the Succession Law of the PRC of 10 April 1985 (effective as of 1 October 1985), which contains a stipulation on the law applicable to the succession of deceased persons (Article 36). But an important legislative document in this area is a statute named the General Principles of Civil Law of the PRC of 12 April 1986 (as modified on 27 August 2009), which entered into effect on 1 January 1987. Chapter VIII, called "Application of Laws to Civil Relationships Involving Foreign Elements" (Articles 142 to 149), contains the first relatively systematic choice-of-law rules in the history of the PRC.

In addition to these pioneering legislative documents, the Rules for Implementation of the Law on Foreign-Capital Enterprises of the PRC issued by the former Ministry of Foreign Economic Relations and Trade on 12 December 1990 (as modified on 12 April 2001, Articles 18, 48-49, 52, 56, 64, 81), the Law on Adoption of the PRC of 29 February 1991 (as modified on 4 November 1998, Article 21), the Maritime Code of the PRC of 7 November 1992 (Articles 268 to 275), the Law on Negotiable Instruments of the PRC of 5 October 1995 (as modified on 28 August 2004, Articles 94-101), the Law on Civil Aviation of the PRC of 30 October 1995 (Articles 185 to 189), the Contract Law of the PRC of 15 March 1999 (Article 126), Measures on the Registration of Adoption of Children by Foreigners in the PRC issued by the Ministry of Civil Affairs on 25 May 1999 (Articles 2 and 3) and the Company Law of the PRC as modified and adopted on 27 October 2005 (Articles 218) all contain choice-of-law rules.[7]

b. Conflict Rules Contained in the Judicial Interpretations of the Supreme People's Court

In China, judicial interpretations of the Supreme Peo-

---

[7] See Chen Weizuo, Bijiao guoji sifa (*Comparative Private International Law*), Tsinghua University Press, Beijing 2008, pp. 439-446; see also Li Shuangyuan, Jiang Xinmiao & Xiong Yuhui, Guanyu qicao woguo guoji sifa fadian de jidian xiangfa (*Some Ideas concerning the Drafting of the Chinese Private International Law Code*), *in Shidai faxue* (*Present-day Law Science*), No. 6/2008, pp. 3-12.

ple's Court are regarded as sources of law. Since 1985, the Supreme People's Court has issued several judicial interpretations containing choice-of-law rules, *e.g.* Opinions of the Supreme People's Court on Several Questions Relating to the Implementation of the Succession Law of the PRC of 9 November 1985 (Article 63); Opinions of the Supreme People's Court on Several Questions Relating to the Implementation of the General Principles of Civil Law of 26 January 1988 (for trial implementation, Articles 179 to 191); [8] Rules of the Supreme People's Court on Several Questions Relating to the Application of Laws in the Trial of Cases of Contractual Disputes in Civil or Commercial Matters Involving Foreign Elements of 11 June 2007 (Article 5).[9]

**4. An Interim Summary of the Necessity of Private International Law Codification from a Historical Perspective**

Despite the above-mentioned choice-of-law rules contained in the present statutes and regulations as well as judicial interpretations, a systematic and comprehensive codification of choice-of-law rules has not been completed in the PRC up until today. From the point of view of historical development, this may be regarded as retrogression when compared with the 1918 Statute on the Application of Laws, the first systematic private international law codification in the

[8] See Huang Jin & Lü Guomin, *New Developments in Chinese Private International Law*, in *Yearbook of Private International Law*, Vol. I (1999), pp. 136-137.

[9] See Zhonghua renmin gongheguo zuigao renmin fayuan gongbao (*Gazette of the Supreme People's Court of the PRC*), No. 9/2007, pp. 6-7.

Chinese legal history. Though promulgated 93 years ago, this Statute contained a number of choice-of-law rules which could be evaluated as advanced in that epoch. The same applies to the 1953 Taiwanese Law on the Application of Laws to Civil Matters Involving Foreign Elements, which has followed the tradition of codification in the field of private international law. Though merely in force in Taiwan, the 1953 Taiwanese Law may be regarded as a positive continuation of Chinese private international law codification effectuated by the 1918 Statute.

However, this tradition of private international law codification has been discontinued by the PRC, in which no systematic and comprehensive private international law codification in a strict sense has been accomplished so far. Indeed, the current Chinese choice-of-law rules are scattered in different legislative documents (statutes and regulations) as well as judicial interpretations pertaining to various aspects of private international law. Without a systemization of choice-of-law rules in the form of a private international law code or a special statute, inconveniences may occur for Chinese judges faced with civil cases involving foreign elements, and injustice may occur for the parties due to the lack of certainty and predictability in the determination of the applicable law.

## C. The Current Necessity of Codification of China's Private International Law and Efforts Thereof

### 1. Reasons for Private International Law Codification in China

According to a study undertaken by the present author, a comprehensive codification of China's private international law is currently justified both in practice and theory of conflicts law, not only from the domestic, but also from the international point of view.

a. Reason for Codification One: Some Current Conflict Rules are Incomplete

Some provisions of the present Chinese statutes and regulations containing conflict rules are incomplete. For example, the General Principles of Civil Law of the PRC contain only 7 conflict rules on a very limited range of topics *i.e.* capability to engage in civil transactions, immovable property ownership, contracts, compensation of damages arising out of torts, marriages between Chinese citizens and foreigners, divorce, maintenance and intestate succession, but other areas of civil relationships like parent-child relationship, guardianship as well as testamentary succession have been left unresolved.

b: Reason for Codification Two: Some Current Conflict Rules Are Insufficient or Out of Date

Some statutory conflict rules are insufficient or even out of date. For example, Article 147 First Half Sentence of the General Principles of Civil Law provides that the marriage between a citizen of the PRC and a foreigner shall be governed by the law of the place of celebration, but it does not provide a sufficient distinction between formal validity and essential validity of marriage. Conflict rules contained in some pioneering statutes like the Succession Law of 1985 and the General Principles of Civil Law of 1986, which came into effect in an earlier period of reform and opening to the outside world, have become partially out-dated.[10]

---

10 *See Wolf, China's Private International Investment Law: One-Way Street into PRC Law?* In *Am.J.Comp.L.*, Vol. 56 (2008), p. 1045.

c. Reason for Codification Three: Some Current Conflict Rules are Contradictory to Each Other

Some statutory conflict rules contradict each other. For example, both Article 36 of the Succession Law and Article 149 of the General Principles of Civil Law provide the law applicable to successions. On the one hand, Article 36 of the Succession Law only applies to the succession of Chinese citizens to properties situated outside China or to foreigners' properties situated within China, as well as to the succession of foreigners to properties situated within China or to properties situated outside China. Such a numeration is insufficient to include all situations of succession involving foreign elements. On the other hand, Article 149 of the General Principles of Civil Law applies generally to intestate succession involving foreign elements. These two provisions have obviously different realms of application. If special rules prevail over general rules (*Lex specialis derogat legi generali.*), then Article 36 of the Succession Law shall be applied; if later rules prevail over earlier rules (*Lex posterior derogat priori.*), then Article 149 of the General Principles of Civil Law shall be applied. But neither legislative interpretations of the Standing Committee of the NPC nor judicial interpretations of the Supreme People's Court have expressed any opinion on this matter.

d. Reason for Codification Four: There are Contradictions between Judicial Interpretations and Statutes

Some conflict rules contained in the judicial interpretations of the Supreme People's Court remain in disharmony with statutory conflict rules. Although it is generally accepted that judicial interpretations have the force of law within the court system of China, the position of the conflict rules contained in the judicial interpretations issued by the Supreme

People's Court, especially in cases where they are contradictory to the statutory conflict rules, is not beyond dispute. Sometimes, the Supreme People's Court produced conflict rules which are much more numerous and more detailed than the conflict rules contained in statutes and regulations. For example, Article 8 of the Rules of the Supreme People's Court on Several Questions Relating to the Application of Laws in the Trial of Cases of Contractual Disputes in Civil or Commercial Matters Involving Foreign Elements of 11 June 2007, which entered into force on 8 August 2007[11], has listed 17 types of contract in civil and commercial matters involving foreign elements, to which the law of the PRC shall be applied. Such unilateral conflict rules in favor of the law of the forum state (*lex fori*) constitute essential limitations of the principle of party autonomy as embodied in Article 145 of the General Principles of Civil Law and Article 126 of the Contract Law. It is unclear whether the Supreme People's Court has been empowered by the NPC, the Chinese supreme legislative body, to issue such conflict rules. If indeed they have been given this mandate, it remains questionable whether conflict rules made by the Supreme People's Court have corresponded with the will of the Chinese legislature.

e. Reason for Codification Five: the Present Chinese Private International Law Lacks Consistent Legislative Technique

A common issue across the reasons articulated above is

[11] *See* Zhonghua renmin gongheguo zuigao renmin fayuan gongbao (*Gazette of the Supreme People's Court of the PRC*), No. 9/2007, pp. 6-7.

the lack of consistent legislative technique in the present Chinese private international law. Some crucial questions of the General Part of private international law *e.g.* characterization, preliminary question, *renvoi*, *ordre public*, the interpretation of applicable law, the application of international treaties, the ascertainment of foreign law as well as a general or exception clause embodying the principle of the closest connection have not been stipulated in a general manner by the present Chinese law.[12] Furthermore, it is unclear which connecting factor (nationality, domicile or habitual residence) has been chosen by the Chinese legislature as the principal connecting factor.

f. Reason for Codification Six: Private International Law Reforms in Foreign Countries as Background of the Private International Law Codification in China

In the last four decades, many countries have codified or reformed their own private international law through enacting choice-of-law rules and relevant rules. Typical examples are private international law codifications in Former Czechoslovakia (1963), Central Africa (1965), Poland (1965), Portugal (1966), Gabon (1972), Spain (1974, 1981 and 1990), Algeria (1975), the Former Democratic Republic of Germany (1975), Austria (1978), Hungary (1979), Former Yugoslavia (1982), Peru (1984), Germany (1986 and 1999), Mexico (1987), Switzerland (1987), Mauritania (1989), the US State of Louisiana (1991), the Province of Québec of Canada (1991), Yemen

[12] *See* Li Shuangyuan, Jiang Xinmiao & Xiong Yuhui, Guanyu qicao woguo guoji sifa fadian de jidian xiangfa (*Some Ideas concerning the Drafting of the Chinese Private International Law Code*), in *Shidai faxue* (*Present-day Law Science*), Vol. 6, No. 6/2008, pp. 3-12.

(1992), Romania (1992), Italy (1995), the Democratic People's Republic of Korea (1995), Lichtenstein (1996), Venezuela (1998), Tunisia (1998), Belarus (1999), the Republic of Korea (2001), Belgium (2004), Bulgaria (2005), Vietnam (2005), Japan (2006) and Turkey (2007).[13]

It is against this background that a general consensus has been reached according to which a systematic and comprehensive private international law codification in a modern and restrictive sense shall be launched and effectuated in China. This has been particularly justified since the accession of the China's membership to the World Trade Organization in 2001. In this time of increasing economic growth and integration into the global economy, China needs to abide by internationally accepted rules of commerce. Modernization of Chinese private international law in the form of codification may be regarded as a step forward.

**2. Efforts of Private International Law Codification in PRC**

Efforts have been made by Chinese scholars to propose the codification of Chinese private international law rules. Several different drafts have been provided by various schol-

---

[13] See Audit, *Droit international privé*, 5e édition, 2008, n° 37; Chen Weizuo, Bijiaofa shiye xia de guoji sifa yuanyuan – jian lun yiban guoji guanli bushi guoji sifa de yuanyuan (*Sources of Private International Law from a Comparative Law Perspective: A Concurrent Discussion on the Proposition that General International Usages are not Sources of Private International Law*), in *Shidai faxue* (*Present-day Law Science*), Vol. 7, No. 5/2009, pp. 81-89.

ars or research groups.[14] One of the drafts was provided by the Chinese Society of Private International Law, whose proposal was the so-called "Model Law of Private International Law of the PRC" circulated in 2000.[15] However, due to its overly wide scope and broad conception of private international law in terms of general provisions, international jurisdiction, application of laws, judicial assistance and supplementary provisions[16], this "model law" did not seem to be seriously considered by the NPC and its Standing Committee. In the case of this particular proposal, it seems that the term "model law" was inappropriately used by some Chinese private international law scholars. As a matter of fact, the proposal was merely a scholarly draft of a private international law statute, not a model law for any country. Had the

[14] A number of conflicts scholars have prepared various versions of private drafts of private international law statute, *e.g.* the draft of a team led by Prof. Zhao Xianglin, the draft of a team led by Prof. Li Shuangyuan, the draft of Prof. Qu Guangqing, the draft of Prof. Chen Xiaoyun etc. See, for example, Li Shuangyuan, Jiang Xinmiao & Xiong Yuhui, Guanyu qicao woguo guoji sifa fadian de jidian xiangfa (*Some Ideas concerning the Drafting of the Chinese Private International Law Code*), in *Shidai faxue* (*Present-day Law Science*), No. 6/2008, pp. 3-12.

[15] Zhongguo guoji sifa xuehui (Chinese Society of Private International Law), Zhonghua renmin gongheguo guojisifa shifanfa (*Model Law of Private International Law of the PRC*), Law Press China, Beijing 2000, pp. 39-86; See also *Yearbook of Private International Law*, Vol. 3 (2001), pp. 283-308.

[16] See Huang Jin & Lü Guomin, *New Developments in Chinese Private International Law*, in *Yearbook of Private International Law*, Vol. I (1999), pp. 155-156.

so-called "model law" hypothetically been adopted, it still would not have been considered a model law even for the two Special Administrative Regions of Hong Kong and Macao, because the PRC is not a federal country like the USA. Neither was the "model law" a model for the Chinese legislature, for the NPC and its Standing Committee have never granted such a mandate. There is, however, room to admit that some provisions contained in this scholarly daft may be useful for the ongoing private international law codification in China.[17]

## D. Arguments for a Statute on the Application of Laws as the Legislative Model

### 1. The Legislative Initiative of Codification of China's Private International Law

In December 2002, the 31st Session of the Standing Committee of the Ninth NPC deliberated on, for the first time, the Draft Civil Code of the PRC, of which Book Nine was entitled "Law on the Application of Laws to Civil Relationships Involving Foreign Elements". The Chinese legislature, which treats private international law as an integral part of the future Chinese civil code, is reluctant to be rushed into drafting the Chinese civil code all at one time. Instead, the Chinese civil code shall be elaborated on the basis of different special statutes in civil matters such as statutes on marriage, succession, adoption, contracts, rights *in rem*, tortious liability and the application of laws to civil relationships involving

[17] See Chen Weizuo, *The Necessity of Codification of China's Private International Law and Arguments for a Statute on the Application of Laws as the Legislative Model*, in *Tsinghua China Law Review*, Vol. 1, No. 1/2009, pp. 5-16.

foreign elements. It is for this reason and against this background that the Statute on the Application of Laws to Civil Relationships Involving Foreign Elements has been put on the agenda by the Chinese legislature.

According to the 2008 Plan for the Legislative Work of the Standing Committee of the NPC adopted on 15 April 2008, the 2008 Arrangement of the Legislative Work contains 12 items of Preparatory Programmes of which the last item is the Statute on the Application of Laws to Civil Relationships Involving Foreign Elements. The Standing Committee of the NPC claimed that "relevant organs are making the best use of their time for survey and study, and for the drafting work. Respective deliberations shall be arranged in 2008 or in the following years."[18] On 15 November 2008, the Legislation Plan of the Standing Committee of the Eleventh NPC was published, containing a catalogue of statutes to be enacted within the present legislative period (2008-2013), among which the Statute on the Application of Laws to Civil Relationships Involving Foreign Elements was listed as one of the six statutes in civil and commercial matters.[19] It is being prepared by the Legislative Affairs Commission of the Standing Committee of the NPC.

During the 16th Session of the Standing Committee of the Eleventh NPC held in Beijing from 23 to 28 August 2010,

[18] See Zhonghua renmin gongheguo quanguo renmin daibiao dahui changwu weiyuanhui gongbao (*Gazette of the Standing Committee of the NPC of the PRC*), No. 4/2008, p. 501.

[19] See Zhonghua renmin gongheguo quanguo renmin daibiao dahui changwu weiyuanhui gongba (*Gazette of the Standing Committee of the NPC of the PRC*), No. 7/2008, pp. 777-778.

the Draft Statute on the Application of Laws to Civil Relationships Involving Foreign Elements was submitted for deliberation. This deliberation was deemed the second deliberation following the preliminary deliberation of Book Nine of the Draft Civil Code of the PRC in December 2002.

Apparently the Chinese legislature has made a decision to first draft a separate statute, exclusively containing choice-of-law rules for the application of laws to civil relationships involving foreign elements. The effort to draft a comprehensive statute containing choice-of-law rules, rules on international jurisdictions and judicial mutual assistance as discussed in the above-mentioned "model law" is no longer being considered.

**2. Possible Legislative Models of the Future China's Private International Law Code and the Legislature's Decision**

In fact, there are three possible legislative models for the Chinese legislature to consider: (a) A code on the application of laws to legal relationships in civil and commercial matters involving foreign elements, which contains exclusively choice-of-law rules, following the legislative model of the Japanese Act on General Rules on the Application of Laws of 15 June 2006; (b) A code containing choice-of-law rules as well as rules on international jurisdiction following the legislative model of the Law on Private International Law of the Republic of Korea of 7 April 2001; (c) A code containing choice-of-law rules as well as rules on international jurisdiction, recognition and enforcement of foreign judgments following the legislative model of the Belgium Code on Private International Law which came into effect on 16 July 2004.

From the above-mentioned legislative programme and

process of the Standing Committee of the NPC, the Chinese legislature has obviously made a decision in favor of the legislative model (a).

The decision of the Standing Committee of the NPC differed from the opinions of some Chinese private international law scholars who were in favor of a comprehensive codification containing choice-of-law rules and relevant rules on international jurisdiction, mutual judicial assistance as shown in the so-called "model law". It may be said that the initiative to achieve a comprehensive statute has failed, but to this author's mind, the Chinese legislature has made a wise choice.

**3. Personal Arguments for a Statute on the Application of Laws**

The legislature's choice is wise because there has been above all a tradition of separate statutes on the application of laws and international civil procedure in the history of modern Chinese law. Both the 1918 Statute on the Application of Laws and the 1953 Taiwanese "Law on the Application of Laws to Civil Matters Involving Foreign Elements" have followed the model of separate codification of choice-of-law rules. Moreover, from a comparative law perspective, countries like Austria, Germany and Japan have all adopted similarly restricted legislative models.

Second, the Chinese legislature has historically been unwilling to adopt a comprehensive statute containing both choice-of-law rules and rules on international civil procedure. In October 2007 the Chinese legislature revised the Civil Procedure Code of 9 April 1991. In this latest reform of Chinese civil procedure law, rules on international jurisdiction and mutual judicial assistance were not treated as objects of modification. Up to now, Chinese courts have applied rules on territorial jurisdiction contained in the Civil Procedure Code of 9 April 1991 by analogy to situations of civil and commercial disputes involving foreign elements.

Third, China is a contracting party of a number of international conventions on international civil procedure including judicial mutual assistance. Rules contained in such international conventions may be directly applied by Chinese judges. On the other hand, very few choice-of-law rules have been found in international conventions of which China is a contracting party. Thus, it is less likely that the Chinese legislature will launch a reform in the field of international civil procedure law in the near future than that they enact a code on conflicts law in the form of a statute on the application of laws to civil relationships involving foreign elements.

Some Chinese scholars are so unrealistic as to include choice-of-law rules and rules on international jurisdiction as well as judicial mutual assistance into one single document. However, their ideas are not likely to be accepted by the Chinese legislature. A separate code exclusively containing choice-of-law rules might be regarded as a more convincing and pragmatic solution by the Chinese legislature. If the Chinese legislature is unsatisfied with its current options regarding codification, the legislative process for the Chinese private international law statute is likely to be largely postponed. This would mean that China would lose its best chance to systemize its choice-of-law rules in a number of years.

## D. Conclusion

Historically, Chinese law has a tradition of written law.

Private international law as a branch of law in the modern sense did not exist in traditional Chinese law. The first systematic codification in this field was the Statute on the Application of Laws of 1918, which ceased to be in the mainland of China after 1949.[20] Although the codification efforts of private international law have sometimes been influenced by political situations and ideological considerations, the historical tradition of codification of Chinese conflicts law since 1918 should not be neglected. As a matter of fact, the 1918 Statute possessed a fairly high level of legislative technique even viewed from present-day's legislative and scientific criteria. We should learn more to draw some lessons from our past experiences of private international law codification both legislatively and scientifically.

The present author is strongly in favor of a separate code containing choice-of-law rules. Nevertheless, despite any legislative model adopted by the Chinese legislature, the future Chinese private international law codification, when determining the applicable law to solve questions of application of laws, shall guarantee a certain level of legal certainty and predictability on the one hand, and necessary flexibility and adaptability on the other hand. The author is convinced that a modern, scientific and successful Chinese private international law codification inspired by internationalism will definitely favor the harmonization of different legal systems be-

---

20 See Herbert Han-Pao Ma, *Private International Law of the Republic of China: Past, Present and the Future*, in *Private Law in the International Arena – Liber Amicorum Kurt Siehr*, T.M.C. Asser Press, 2000, pp. 414-416.

tween China and other countries.[21]

## III. Chinese Private International Law Statute of 28 October 2010: the First PIL Codification in the Legislative History of the PRC [22]

The Statute on the Application of Laws to Civil Relationships Involving Foreign Elements of the PRC (hereinafter referred to as "the Chinese PIL Statute") was adopted on 28 October 2010 during the 17th Session of the Standing Committee of the Eleventh NPC. It entered into force on 1 April 2011. It is the first private international law (hereinafter referred to as "PIL") codification that takes the form of a special statute containing conflict rules (choice-of-law rules) in the 62 years of legislative history of the PRC. The author provides a short comment on the legislative history of the Chinese PIL Statute and its main novelties for the Chinese PIL system. Finally, the author exercises criticism on the Chinese PIL Statute.

### A. Legislative History of the Chinese PIL Statute

In December of 2002, the 31st Session of the Standing

---

[21] See Chen Weizuo, *The Necessity of Codification of China's Private International Law and Arguments for a Statute on the Application of Laws as the Legislative Model*, in *Tsinghua China Law Review*, Vol. 1, No. 1/2009, pp. 17-20.

[22] The content of this section is to be published in *Yearbook of Private International Law*, Vol. XII (2010), sellier. european law publishers, 2011.

Committee of the Ninth NPC deliberated for the first time on the Draft Civil Code of the PRC. Part Nine of the Draft Civil Code was entitled "Application of Laws to Civil Relationships Involving Foreign Elements". However, the Chinese legislature, which treated conflict rules as an integral part of the future Chinese civil code, was reluctant to be rushed into drafting the entire Chinese civil code all at once. Instead, the Chinese civil code has since been developed on the basis of different special statutes on civil matters, such as statutes on marriage, succession, adoption, contracts, rights *in rem*, tortious liability and the application of laws to civil relationships involving foreign elements. For this reason the Statute on the Application of Laws to Civil Relationships Involving Foreign Elements was put on the agenda of several sessions of the Standing Committee of the NPC.

According to the 2008 Plan for the Legislative Work of the Standing Committee of the NPC adopted on 15 April 2008, the 2008 Arrangement for the Legislative Work contained 12 items of preparatory programmes, the last of which was the Statute on the Application of Laws to Civil Relationships Involving Foreign Elements. The Standing Committee of the NPC claimed in 2008 that "the relevant organs are making the best use of their time for survey and study, and for the drafting work. Respective deliberations shall be arranged in 2008 or in the following years."[23] On 15 November 2008, the Legislation Programme of the Standing Committee of the Eleventh NPC was published, containing a

---

[23] See Zhonghua renmin gongheguo quanguo renmin daibiao dahui changwu weiyuanhui gongbao (*Gazette of the Standing Committee of the NPC of the PRC*), No. 4/2008, p. 501.

catalogue of statutes to be enacted within the present legislative period (2008-2013), among which the Statute on the Application of Laws to Civil Relationships Involving Foreign Elements was listed as one of the six statutes on civil and commercial matters.[24] The Legislative Affairs Commission of the Standing Committee of the NPC became the organ that prepared the Draft Statute on the Application of Laws to Civil Relationships Involving Foreign Elements for consideration.

According to the 2010 Plan for the Legislative Work of the Standing Committee of the NPC published on 1 April 2010[25], 2010 was to be a key year for shaping "the socialist system of law with Chinese characteristics". Hence, it was necessary to enact those statutes playing a supporting role in "the socialist system of law with Chinese characteristics", and to promote "scientific legislation" and "democratic legislation", so as to realize the legislative objectives. Nine legislative bills were arranged to be further deliberated on by the Standing Committee of the NPC in 2010 (since they had previously been deliberated on once or twice), among which the Draft Statute on the Application of Laws to Civil Relationships Involving Foreign Elements was eighth on the list.

Following adoption of the Statute on Tortious Liability of the PRC on 26 December 2009, the Civil Law Section of

---

[24] See Zhonghua renmin gongheguo quanguo renmin daibiao dahui changwu weiyuanhui gongbao (*Gazette of the Standing Committee of the NPC of the PRC*), No. 7/2008, pp. 777-778.

[25] See Zhonghua renmin gongheguo quanguo renmin daibiao dahui changwu weiyuanhui gongbao (*Gazette of the Standing Committee of the NPC of the PRC*), No. 4/2010, pp. 359-360.

the Legislative Affairs Commission of the Standing Committee of the NPC began to elaborate, at the beginning of 2010, on the Draft Statute on the Application of Laws to Civil Relationships Involving Foreign Elements. The result was the Draft Statute for Amendment of 28 June 2010 that contained 8 chapters and 60 articles. The Civil Law Section of the Legislative Affairs Commission has invited PIL experts[26], including the present author, to participate in a legislative symposium held at the Conference Centre of the NPC in Beijing from 30 June to 1 July 2010. The experts made a number of suggestions for amendment to, and further development of, the Draft Statute. Later, on 17 August 2010, an experts' meeting on the Draft Statute was held by the Legislative Affairs Commission, in which the present author also participated. Consensus was reached between the 6 participating PIL experts[27] and the Legislative Affairs Commission with

[26] Huang Jin (China University of Political Science and Law), Fei Zongyi (Supreme People's Court), Liu Huishan (Foreign Affairs University), Zhao Xianglin (China University of Political Science and Law), Lu Song (Foreign Affairs University), Ding Wei (East China University of Political Science and Law), Xiao Yongping (Wuhan University), Guo Yujun (Wuhan University), Song Lianbin (Wuhan University), N.N. (Zhongnan University of Economics and Law), Wang Jun (University of Foreign Economics and Trade), Du Tao (Fudan University) and Chen Weizuo (Tsinghua University).

[27] Huang Jin (China University of Political Science and Law), Fei Zhongyi (Supreme People's Court), Liu Huishan (Foreign Affairs University), Jiang Rujiao (China University of Political Science and Law), Chen Weizuo (Tsinghua University) and Du Huanfang (Renmin University).

regard to the principal connecting factor of the Draft Statute (habitual residence), the law applicable to legal capacity and capacity to engage in juristic acts of natural persons, the law applicable to a declaration of a missing person and a declaration of death of a natural person, the law applicable to essential conditions to marriage, and the law applicable to personal and property relationships between spouses. The Law Committee of the NPC held a meeting on the same day and reviewed the Draft Statute. On this basis, the Draft Statute was submitted for deliberation during the 16th Session of the Standing Committee of the Eleventh NPC held in Beijing from 23 to 28 August 2010. From a legislative perspective, this was deemed the second deliberation following the preliminary deliberation of Part Nine of the Draft Civil Code in December 2002. In reality, this was the first essential deliberation of the Draft Statute, since Part Nine of the Draft Civil Code had not been seriously deliberated on due to the fact that from December 2002 to December 2009 focus had been directed toward drafting the Statute on Rights *in Rem* and the Statute on Tortious Liability that were adopted in March 2007 and December 2009, respectively.

After the second deliberation during the 16th Session of the Standing Committee of the Eleventh NPC, the Draft Statute was published on the website of the NPC for criticism and proposals.[28] Compared with the Draft for Amendment of 28 June 2010, the Draft Statute for Second Deliberation was abridged to 54 articles from the original 60. On 16 Sep

[28] http://www.npc.gov.cn/huiyi/lfzt/swmsgxflsyf/node_14074.htm.

tember 2010, the Legislative Affairs Commission of the Standing Committee of the NPC again solicited 5 PIL experts[29], including the present author, for their opinions, primarily on the law applicable to intellectual property rights. Meanwhile, the Standing Committee of the NPC had gathered several hundred comments and criticisms from the general public across China. The Law Committee of the NPC prepared the Draft Statute of 14 October 2010 containing 51 articles and further submitted it to the 17th Session of the Standing Committee of the Eleventh NPC, held from 25 to 28 October 2010, for the third deliberation. Several amendments were made, particularly Article 18 on the law applicable to arbitration agreements, which was added at the last moment of the third deliberation. The final version of the Statute was adopted on 28 October 2010, and contained 8 chapters and 52 articles.

The adoption of the Chinese PIL Statute marked the realization of the legislative objective set by the Legislation Programme of the Standing Committee of the Eleventh NPC and the 2010 Plan for the Legislative Work.

## B. Main Novelties of the Chinese PIL Statute for the Chinese PIL System

### 1. Systemization and Modernization of Chinese Conflict Rules

The Chinese PIL Statute has systemized and modernized Chinese Conflict Rules. Until adoption of the Chinese

[29] Huang Jin (China University of Political Science and Law), Fei Zhongyi (Supreme People's Court), Liu Huishan (Foreign Affairs University), Chen Weizuo (Tsinghua University) and Xu Xiang (Wuhan University).

PIL Statute, Chinese statutory conflict rules were mainly contained in Chapter VIII of the General Principles of Civil Law of the PRC of 12 April 1986 (as modified on 27 August 2009), "Application of Laws to Civil Relationships Involving Foreign Elements" (Articles 142 to 149), and other statutes and regulations.[30] In addition, conflict rules were also contained in several judicial interpretations issued by the Supreme Peo-

[30] Such as: the Succession Law of the PRC of 10 April 1985 (Article 36), the Rules for Implementation of the Law on Foreign-Capital Enterprises of the PRC issued by the former Ministry of Foreign Economic Relations and Trade on 12 December 1990 (as modified on 12 April 2001, Articles 18, 48-49, 52, 56, 64 and 81), the Law on Adoption of the PRC of 29 February 1991 (as modified on 4 November 1998, Article 21), the Maritime Code of the PRC of 7 November 1992 (Articles 268 to 275), the Law on Negotiable Instruments of the PRC of 5 October 1995 (as modified on 28 August 2004, Articles 94-101), the Law on Civil Aviation of the PRC of 30 October 1995 (Articles 185 to 189), the Contract Law of the PRC of 15 March 1999 (Article 126), Measures on the Registration of Adoption of Children by Foreigners in the PRC issued by the Ministry of Civil Affairs on 25 May 1999 (Articles 2 and 3) and the Company Law of the PRC as modified and adopted on 27 October 2005 (Articles 218). See Chen Weizuo, Bijiao guoji sifa (*Comparative Private International Law*), Tsinghua University Press, Beijing 2008, pp. 439-446.

ple's Court.[31] However, prior to the Chinese PIL Statute provisions of Chinese statutes and regulations containing conflict rules were incomplete. Some statutory conflict rules were insufficient or out of date and some even contradicted one another. Also, other conflict rules contained in the judicial interpretations of the Supreme People's Court were incompatible with statutory conflict rules. Finally, Chinese PIL lacked a consistent legislative technique. Therefore, a comprehensive codification of Chinese PIL rules was necessary.[32]

The Chinese PIL Statute contains the following 8 chapters: Chapter I (General Provisions, Articles 1-10), Chapter II (Civil Subjects, Articles 11-20), Chapter III (Marriage and Family, Articles 21-30), Chapter IV (Succession, Articles 31-35), Chapter V (Rights *in Rem*, Articles 36-40), Chapter VI

---

[31] Such as: the Opinions of the Supreme People's Court on Several Questions Relating to the Implementation of the Succession Law of the PRC of 9 November 1985 (Article 63), the Opinions of the Supreme People's Court on Several Questions Relating to the Implementation of the General Principles of Civil Law of 26 January 1988 (for trial implementation, Articles 179 to 191) and the Rules of the Supreme People's Court on Several Questions Relating to the Application of Laws in the Trial of Cases of Contractual Disputes in Civil or Commercial Matters Involving Foreign Elements of 11 June 2007 (Article 5). See Huang Jin & Lü Guomin, *New Developments in Chinese Private International Law*, in *Yearbook of Private International Law*, Vol. I (1999), pp. 136-137.

[32] See Chen Weizuo, *The Necessity of Codification of China's Private International Law and Arguments for a Statute on the Application of Laws as the Legislative Model*, in *Tsinghua China Law Review*, Vol. 1, No. 1/2009, pp. 1-20.

(Creditors' Rights, Articles 41-47), Chapter VII (Intellectual Property Rights, Articles 48-50) and Chapter VIII (Supplementary Provisions, Articles 51-52). For the first time in the history of the PRC, systematized conflict rules have been contained in a single special statute stipulating the applicable law to various legal relationships in civil matters involving foreign elements. Judging from their content, these new conflict rules are more reasonable and more complete. They result from experiences of civil trials involving foreign elements since the time of China's reform and opening to the outside world. At the same time, they are adapted to the trends of development for contemporary PIL.

**2. Habitual Residence as the Principal Connecting Factor**

The Chinese PIL Statute has creatively chosen habitual residence as the principal connecting factor for determining the applicable law. Accordingly, habitual residence plays a decisive role in determining the law applicable to legal relationships in civil matters relating to personal status and capacity, marriage, family and succession. In comparative PIL, jurisdictions having a civil law tradition generally follow the nationality principle, whereas jurisdictions having a common law tradition generally follow the domicile principle. However, both nationality and domicile have their own defects and limitations. Since the Convention of 24 October 1956 on the Law Applicable to Maintenance Obligations Towards Children[33], the Hague Conference on Private International Law has

---

[33] *Convention du 24 octobre 1956 sur la loi applicable aux obligations alimentaires envers les enfants.* English translation in Am.J.Comp.L. 656 (1956).

abandoned the nationality principle followed by the early Hague Conventions, and has given preference to habitual residence. The practice of the Hague Conference has greatly influenced many countries' PIL legislation. This is also reflected in the Chinese PIL Statute, which treats habitual residence in a unique manner. Ordinarily, the applicable law determined in accordance with the Chinese PIL Statute is the law of the place of habitual residence. If the law of the place of habitual residence is to be applied according to the Chinese PIL Statute, and if the place of habitual residence of a natural person is unknown, the law of the place of his/her actual residence shall be applied (Article 20). For a legal person, the place of habitual residence is its principal place of business (Article 14, Paragraph II, Sentence 2). From the present author's perspective, the choice of habitual residence as the principal connecting factor in the Chinese PIL Statute coincides with trends of globalization: Foreign and domestic natural and legal persons are undertaking civil transactions with increasing frequency. Moreover, habitual residence is normally the centre of gravity for one person's life and in many cases, the place where the bulk of his/her property is situated.

**3. Role of the Principle of the Closest Connection**

The principle of the closest connection plays a role in the Chinese PIL Statute. Article 2, Paragraph II provides: "If the present Statute or other statutes contain no provisions with regard to the application of laws to civil relationships involving foreign elements, the law that has the closest connection with the civil relationship involving foreign elements shall be applied." The fact that the principle of the closest connection appears in the General Part has already made this principle conspicuous. Nevertheless, neither has the Chinese PIL Statute treated the principle of the closest connection as the "principle of the strongest relationship", like Article 1 of the Austrian Federal Statute on Private International Law (IPR-Gesetz) of 15 June 1978, nor has it treated the principle of the closest connection as an exception clause, like Article 15, Paragraph I of the Swiss Federal Statute on Private International Law (IPRG) of 18 December 1987. In reality, the Chinese PIL Statute treats the principle of the closest connection as a mere supplementary principle. If the Chinese PIL Statute and other Chinese statutes contain no provisions on the law applicable to civil relationships involving foreign elements, or if the law applicable to a certain civil relationship involving foreign elements cannot be determined according to those statutes, the principle of the closest connection may play a supplementing role. In the Special Part of the Chinese PIL Statute, Article 41, on the law applicable to contracts, expressly treats the principle of the closest connection as the criterion of application of laws secondary to the principle of party autonomy. The same article has also expressly listed "the law of the place of habitual residence of one party whose performance of obligations can best embody the characteristics of the contract" as one of "the laws that have the closest connection with the contract". Thus, it has introduced the doctrine of "characteristic performance" into Chinese PIL legislation. In the General Part, if a civil relationship involving foreign elements is to be governed by foreign law, and if different regions in the foreign country have different laws in force, the law of the region with which the civil relationship involving foreign elements has the closest connection shall be applied (Article 6). If the law of the country of nationality is to be applied according to the Chinese PIL Statute, and a natural person has two or more nationalities, the law of the country of nationality in which he/she has a habitual residence shall be applied; if he/she has no habitual residence in any country of nationality, the law of the country of nationality with which he/she has the closest connection shall be applied (Article 19, Sentence 1).

**4. Role of the Principle of Party Autonomy**

The Chinese PIL Statute has given a conspicuous position to the principle of party autonomy. Article 3 provides: "In accordance with statutory provisions, the parties may expressly choose the law applicable to a civil relationship involving foreign elements." Though it is only a declarative clause, the fact that it has embodied the principle of party autonomy in the General Part itself is a emphasis of this principle, with a guiding significance for the people's courts, administrative organs and arbitration institutions, and also playing a guiding role for the Chinese PIL Statute as a whole. In the Special Part, apart from the traditional conflict rule applying the principle of party autonomy to contractual matters (Article 41), the following all allow the parties to choose the applicable law: (1) Article 16, Paragraph II on the law applicable to an entrusted agency; (2) Article 17 on the law applicable to a trust; (3) Article 18 on the law applicable to an arbitration agreement; (4) Article 24 on the law applicable to property relationships of spouses; (5) Article 26 on the law applicable to divorce by agreement; (6) Article 37 on the law applicable to rights *in rem* of movable property; (7) Article 38 on the law applicable to rights *in rem* of movable property that change during transport; (8) Article 44, Sentence 2 on the choice of the applicable law by the parties after occurrence of a tortious act; (9) Article 47 on the law applicable to unjust enrichment or *negotiorum gestio*; (10) Article 49 on the law applicable to the transfer and licensed use of intellectual property rights; and (11) Article 50 on the law applicable to tortious liability arising out of infringement of intellectual property rights. In summary, as long as the choice of the applicable law by the parties takes place "in accordance with statutory provisions", *i.e.* within the limits permitted by the Chinese PIL Statute and other Chinese statutes, the parties may always choose the applicable law by express agreement. The Chinese PIL Statute shows a remarkable open-mindedness in this respect.

**5. Protection of the Weaker Party**

The Chinese PIL Statute aims to protect the interests of socially and economically weaker parties. In the absence of a place of common habitual residence, personal and property relationships between parent and child is governed by the law of the place of habitual residence or the law of the country of nationality of one party, provided that it is the law favoring protection of the rights and interests of the weaker party (Article 25). Likewise, maintenance is governed by the law of the place of habitual residence or the law of the country of nationality of one party, or the law of the place where the principal property is situated, provided that it is the law favoring protection of the rights and interests of the person to be maintained (Article 29). Guardianship is governed by the law of the place of habitual residence or the law of the country of nationality of one party, provided that it is the law favoring protection of the rights and interests of the ward (Article 30). In addition, "the law of the place of the consumer's habitual residence" under the opening half-sentence of Article 42 generally favours the protection of the rights and interests of consumers, "the law of the place where the laborer works" under Article 43, Sentence 1 generally favours the protection of the rights and interests of laborers, and "the law of the place of habitual residence of the person whose right has been infringed upon" under Articles 45 and 46 generally favours the protection of the rights and interests of persons whose rights have been infringed upon. This is because the law of the place of habitual residence of the weaker party and "the law of the place where the laborer works" are frequently the legal systems that are the most familiar to the weaker parties, and also the legal systems upon which they may base their claims.[34]

**6. Equal Treatment of Foreign and Domestic Legal Systems**

All the conflict rules contained in the Chinese PIL Statute are bilateral (multilateral) conflict rules. They reflect the open-mindedness of the Chinese legislator, who treats domestic and foreign legal systems equally. Taking a sweeping view of all the articles of the Chinese PIL Statute, there are only two that expressly provide that "the law of the PRC shall be applied". Those are Article 5 on the application of a foreign law that would cause harm to social and public interests of the PRC, and Article 10, Paragraph II on the applicable law where the law of a foreign country cannot be ascertained, or if the law of that country contains no relevant provisions. However, these are in fact not conflict rules and therefore are

---

34 See Chen Weizuo, Shewai minshi falüshiyongfa de lifa sikao (*Some Legislative Considerations on the Chinese Statute on the Application of Laws in Civil Matters Involving Foreign Elements*), in *Tsinghua Law Journal*, No. 3/2010, p. 118.

not unilateral conflict rules. This is to be welcomed. For Chinese organs (the people's courts, administrative organs or arbitration institutions) exercising international jurisdiction, the application of foreign laws could be not only necessary but also justified and appropriate. In contrast, unilateralism in favor of the application of Chinese law could lead to consequences that are unjustified and inconvenient to the parties. Through enactment of bilateral conflict rules which not only designate Chinese law, but also designate foreign laws as applicable, the Chinese legislator makes clear that if a foreign legal system has the closest connection with cases, and if its application does not cause harm to Chinese social and public interests, the application of that foreign law satisfies the intention of the legislator and may even be understood as an express order given by the legislator to the Chinese organs exercising international jurisdiction.[35]

**7. Structure of the Chinese PIL Statute and Some Characteristics of the General Part**

The Chinese PIL Statute contains a general part (general provisions), a special part and supplementary provisions. Chapter I, "General Provisions" (Articles 1 to 10), forms the General Part, while Chapters II to VII (Articles 11 to 50) form the Special Part, which stipulates special conflict rules on the determination of the law applicable to various civil relationships involving foreign elements (civil subjects, marriage and family, succession, rights *in rem*, obligations and intellectual property rights). Chapter VIII (supplementary provisions) includes Article 51 on the relationship between the

[35] See Chen Weizuo, Bijiao guoji sifa (*Comparative Private International Law*), Tsinghua University Press, Beijing 2008, pp. 107-108.

Chinese PIL Statute and other statutes and Article 52 on the date of entry into force of the Chinese PIL Statute.

One characteristic of the Chinese PIL Statute is inclusion of ten general provisions articles in Chapter I, which serve to remedy China's lack of PIL general provisions and institutions. Thus the legislative gap has been filled. According to Article 8, the characterization of any civil relationship involving foreign elements shall be undertaken in accordance with the *lex fori*. This coincides with the practice of the majority of countries since the "discovery" of the characterization problem by the German Franz Kahn (1861-1904) and the Frenchman Etienne Bartin (1860-1948) at the end of the 19th century. Article 9 of the Chinese PIL Statute excludes all forms of *renvoi* (remission and transmission). This is justified because the principal connecting factor of the Chinese PIL Statute is habitual residence instead of nationality, and the exclusion of *renvoi* serves to increase legal certainty and predictability. In comparative PIL, the following jurisdictions also exclude *renvoi* in their PIL legislation: Argentina, Armenia, Egypt, Brazil, Denmark, Peru, Québec (Canada), Lithuania, Somalia, Tadzhikistan and Greece.[36] According to Article 5 of the Chinese PIL Statute, if the application of a foreign law would cause harm to social and public interests of the PRC, the foreign law that is normally applicable under a conflict rule of the Chinese PIL Statute shall be excluded; instead, the law of the PRC shall be applied. This *ordre public* clause has a formulation that is much better than the one in Article 150 of

---

[36] See Weizuo CHEN, *Rück- und Weiterverweisung (Renvoi) in staatsvertraglichen Kollisionsnormen*, Peter Lang Europäischer Verlag der Wissenschaft, Frankfurt am Main 2004, p. 42.

the General Principles of Civil Law, Article 276 of the Maritime Code, and Article 190 of the Law on Civil Aviation. Finally, Article 10 on the ascertainment of foreign law provides for ascertainment of the governing foreign law by the people's courts, administrative organs and arbitration institutions in principle. In case of a choice of foreign law by the parties, information on the foreign law is to be provided by the parties.

### 8. *Loi d'application immédiate* of the Forum State

For the first time under Chinese law, the Chinese PIL Statute explicitly provides the immediate application of rules of *loi d'application immédiate* of the forum state to civil relationships involving foreign elements. These are mandatory substantive rules of the forum state that have to be directly or exclusively applied by the courts or other organs dealing with international cases due to their special objectives. Article 4 of the Chinese PIL Statute provides: "If the law of the PRC contains mandatory rules on civil relationships involving foreign elements, those mandatory rules shall be applied directly." Because of their mandatory nature, such rules of Chinese law prevail over conflict rules contained in the Chinese PIL Statute. They are to be immediately applied by Chinese organs exercising international jurisdiction, since their sphere of application has been defined by the Chinese legislator, and they are intended to be applied directly to some civil relationships involving foreign elements.[37]

---

[37] See Chen Weizuo, Shewai minshi falüshiyongfa de lifa sikao (*Some Legislative Considerations on the Chinese Statute on the Application of Laws in Civil Matters Involving Foreign Elements*), in *Tsinghua Law Journal*, No. 3/2010, p. 124.

9. Transitory Law and Relations with Conflict Rules Contained in Other Statutes

The Chinese PIL Statute has partly resolved the question of transitory law and the question of relations with conflict rules contained in other Chinese statutes.

With regard to transitory law, the Chinese PIL Statute is applicable to civil relationships involving foreign elements that occur after the date of its entry into force (1 April 2011), whereas civil relationships involving foreign elements that have occurred prior to this date shall still be governed by Chapter VIII of the General Principles of Civil Law and other statutes, regulations and judicial interpretations containing conflict rules, because under Article 84 of the Legislation Law of the PRC, Chinese statutes are generally not retroactively applied.

As to the relation between the conflict rules contained in the Chinese PIL Statute and conflict rules contained in other Chinese special statutes, Article 2, Paragraph I, Sentence 2 provides: "If other statutes contain special provisions on the application of laws to civil relationships involving foreign elements, those provisions shall prevail." This provision coincides with the principle embodied in Article 83 of the Legislation Law of the PRC, *i.e.*, if there is inconsistency between special provisions and general provisions, the special provisions shall prevail. However, if the Chinese legislator does not express an opinion on the question of whether conflict rules contained in statutes, regulations and judicial interpretations that are in force prior to the entry into force of the Chinese PIL Statute shall prevail, there will still be conflicts between new and old conflict rules. For this reason, Article 51 of the Chinese PIL Statute provides that where Articles 146 and 147 of the General Principles of Civil Law and Article 36 of the Succession Law differ from the provisions of the Chinese PIL Statute, the Chinese PIL Statute shall be applied.

In addition, the Chinese legislator has decided not to include conflict rules for commercial matters into the Chinese PIL Statute. In a report on the Draft Statute the Law Committee of the NPC pointed out that conflict rules for commercial matters were to be prescribed in special statutes.[38]

**10. Relationship between Legal Certainty and Flexibility**

The Chinese PIL Statute has dealt with the relationship between legal certainty and flexibility. Like legislators of many countries having a civil law tradition, the Chinese legislator has paid great attention to legal certainty and predictability, for the majority of conflict rules contained in the Chinese PIL Statute are so-called "jurisdiction-selecting rules". Meanwhile the Chinese legislator has also paid attention to flexibility in the determination of applicable laws.

One of the methods to increase flexibility employed by the Chinese PIL Statute is the adoption of the principle of the closest connection. Examples may be found in Article 6 in the General Part as well as Article 19, Sentence 1, Article 39

[38] See Hu Kangsheng, Quanguo renmin daibiao dahui falü weiyuanhui guanyu zhonghua renmin gongheguo shewai minshi guanxi falü shiyongfa (cao'an) zhuyao wenti de huibao (*Report by the Law Commission of the NPC on Major Problems of the Draft Statute on the Application of Laws to Civil Relationships Involving Foreign Elements of the PRC*), in Zhonghua renmin gongheguo quanguo renmin daibiao dahui changwu weiyuanhui gongbao (*Gazette of the Standing Committee of the NPC of the PRC*), No. 7/2010, pp. 643-645.

and Article 41, Sentence 2 in the Special Part. Using as a connecting factor the place having the closest connection may itself overcome the rigidity of Savigny's traditional conflict rules.

The second method to increase legal flexibility employed by the Chinese PIL Statute is to provide some optional conflict rules. For example, matters relating to a legal person are generally governed by the law of the place of registration of a legal person (Article 14, Paragraph I). However, if the principal place of business of the legal person differs from the place of registration, the law of the principal place of business may be applied (Article 14, Paragraph II, Sentence 1). This means, in case of a difference between the principal place of business of a legal person and the place of registration, Chinese organs exercising international jurisdiction may apply either the law of the principal place of business or the law of the place of registration. Similar examples can be found in Article 43, Sentence 1 and Article 50, in which a certain legal system "may be applied" or a certain civil relationship "may be governed by" a legal system, or "the parties may also choose by agreement" a certain legal system as applicable.

The third method to increase flexibility employed by the Chinese PIL Statute is to determine the law applicable to various civil relationships on the basis of a large number of subsidiary connecting factors. Apart from habitual residence, the following subsidiary connecting factors are also used by the Chinese PIL Statute: (1) the place of actual residence; (2) nationality; (3) the place of act; (4) the place of the act of agency; (5) the place where the marriage is celebrated; (6) the place of the act of testament; (7) the place of the tortious act; (8) the place of registration; (9) the principal place of business;

(10) the place where the principal property is situated; (11) the place where the immovable property is situated; (12) the place where the movable property is situated; (13) the place where the estates are situated; (14) the place where the trust property is situated; (15) the place where the trust relationship occurs; (16) the place where the agency relationship occurs; (17) the place of forum; (18) the place where the arbitration institution is situated; (19) the place of arbitration; (20) the place where the institution conducting the divorce formalities is situated; (21) the place of transport destination; (22) the place where the rights of the securities are realized; (23) the place where the pledge is established; (24) the place of the provision of commodities or services; (25) the place where the laborer works; (26) the labor dispatching place; (27) the place where the injury occurs; (28) the place of occurrence of the unjust enrichment or *negotiorum gestio*; (29) the place for which the protection is invoked; (30) the place of the closest connection; and (31) the place chosen by the parties. These numerous subsidiary connecting factors reflect the plurality of civil relationships as well as the complexity of civil disputes in the context of globalization as well as internal requirements of flexibility in determining the governing law.

## C. Criticism

Despite the above-mentioned novelties, there are still a number of defects - even mistakes - in the Chinese PIL Statute.

Firstly, the titles of several chapters are not completely logical. Chapter II is entitled "Civil Subjects", but actually contains rules on natural persons and legal persons. It would be more accurate if entitled "Natural Persons and Legal Persons". Chapter VI is entitled "Creditors' Rights" which is also inaccurate: This chapter mainly deals with contractual obligations and non-contractual obligations. It would be more accurate if entitled "Obligations" or "Law of Obligations". Moreover, the position of Chapter VI between the chapters on rights *in rem* and intellectual property rights is illogical. A better sequence would be Chapter V "Obligations" (or "Law of Obligations"), Chapter VI "Rights *in Rem*" followed by Chapter VII "Intellectual Property Rights".

Secondly, the governing law designated by the Chinese PIL Statute has been frequently formulated as "the law of the place of…" which is not accurate. As a matter of fact, the main objective of the Chinese PIL Statute should be determination of the law applicable to various civil relationships involving foreign elements. The majority of the conflict rules of the Chinese PIL Statute take the form of classical "jurisdiction-selecting rules", in which the legal system of a certain jurisdiction (such as a country) is to be chosen as the governing law, regardless of the concrete content of the legal system of this jurisdiction (especially country). Precisely speaking, what is to be chosen is not the legal system itself, but the very jurisdiction (or country). Unfortunately, the Chinese legislator has ignored the fact that "country" or "jurisdiction" should be mentioned here. Consequently, the majority of the conflict rules contained in the Chinese PIL Statute speak of "the law of the place of…" (*e.g.* the law of the place of habitual residence, the law of the principal place of business, the law of the place of registration, the law of the place where the immovable property is situated etc). However, these are not the best expressions. It would be more fitting to formulate them as the law of the country of habitual residence, the law of the country of principal place of business, the law of the country of registration, the law of the country in which the immovable property is situated, etc. Besides, in some articles the law of the *place* of habitual residence and the law of the *country* of nationality of one party (see Articles 25, 29 and 30) are listed together. In such circumstances, it would be more accurate to speak of the law of the country of habitual residence.

Thirdly, ambiguity or lack of clarity exists in the Chinese PIL Statute. For example, "the law of the place where the principal property is situated" in Article 29 is unclear. The question is: Whose main property shall be decisive for determining the applicable law? No clear answer may be drawn from the text of the Chinese PIL Statute. Another example is Article 25 which, in its original Chinese text, speaks of "the weak party". This should be modified as "the weaker party".

Fourthly, some conflict rules are unnecessary. For example, Article 43, Sentence 2 provides for a conflict rule on labor dispatch which shall be governed by the law of the dispatching place. The present author personally holds that such a provision is completely unnecessary, because labor dispatch is neither an independent type of civil relationship involving foreign elements nor a type of civil dispute in Chinese judicial practice. The same applies to Article 15 on the law applicable to contents of rights of personality and Article 40 on the law applicable to pledge of rights.

Fifthly, some articles are probably mistaken. For example, Article 37, Sentence 1 provides that the parties may choose by agreement the law applicable to rights *in rem* of movable property; Sentence 2 provides that in the absence of a choice by the parties, the law of the place where the movable property is situated at the time of the occurrence of the juristic fact concerned shall be applied. These provisions subject rights *in rem* of movable property primarily to the legal system of a country as chosen by the parties by agreement. Yet it may be wrong to do so. Perhaps the Chinese legislator mistakenly thought that the law applicable to rights *in rem* could be freely chosen by the parties, ignoring the fact that rights *in rem* are different from contractual and non-contractual obligations, and require different conflict rules from those relating to the law applicable to obligations. As a matter of fact, PIL systems of most countries subject both rights *in rem* of immovable property and movable property to the law of the country where the property is situated (*lex loci situs*), whereas the acquisition, loss, change and exercise of rights *in rem* of movable property are generally subjected to the law of the country where the property is situated at the time of the event giving rise to the acquisition, loss, change and exercise.[39] Moreover, Article 38, Sentence 1 provides that the parties may choose by agreement the law applicable to rights *in rem* of movable property that change during transport. This provision does not make sense. There have been enormous difficulties for the present author to translate the original text of Article 38, Sentence 1 into foreign languages. We have to wait and see what the Chinese

[39] See, *e.g.* Article 100 Paragraph I of the Swiss Federal Statute on Private International Law (IPRG) of 18 December 1987 9, Article 31 of the Austrian Federal Statute on Private International Law (IPR-Gesetz) of 15 June 1978, Article 24 of the Polish Statute on Private International Law of 12 November 1965 and Article 13 Article of the Japanese Act on the General Rules of the Application of Laws of 15 June 2006.

legislator really intended as the meaning of this provision.

Although there are still some defects or errors, the Chinese PIL Statute will greatly enhance the certainty, predictability and flexibility in determining the law applicable to various civil relationships involving foreign elements. The modernization of Chinese PIL legislation is to be regarded as an integral part of the global movement of PIL codification since the 1960s. It is China's contribution to the harmonization of different PIL systems in various countries.

# Addendum 1 Chinese Statutory Conflict Rules and Conflict Rules Contained in Judicial Interpretations Prior to 1 April 2011

**The Succession Law of the PRC of 10 April 1985**, Article 36: "(1) For inheritance by a Chinese citizen of an estate outside the PRC or of an estate of a foreigner within the PRC, the law of domicile of the decedent shall be applied in the case of movable property; in the case of immovable property, the law of the place where the property is situated shall be applied. (2) For inheritance by a foreigner of an estate within the PRC or of an estate of a Chinese citizen outside the PRC, the law of domicile of the decedent shall be applied in the case of movable property; in the case of immovable property, the law of the place where the immovable property is situated shall be applied. (3) Where treaties or agreements exist between the PRC and foreign countries, matters of inheritance shall be handled in accordance with such treaties or agreements."

**The General Principles of Civil Law of the PRC of 12 April 1986 (as modified on 27 August 2009)**, Article 142: "The application of laws to civil relationships involving foreign elements shall be determined by the provisions in this Chapter. If any international treaty concluded or acceded to by the PRC contains provisions differing from those in the civil law statutes of the PRC, the provisions of the international treaty shall be applied, unless the provisions are ones on which the PRC has announced reservations. International usages may be applied on matters for which neither the law of the PRC nor any international treaty concluded or acceded to by the PRC has any provisions." Article 143: "If a citizen of the PRC settles in a foreign country, the law of that country may be applicable as regards his capacity to engage in civil transactions." Article 144: "The ownership of immovable property shall be governed by the law of the place where the immovable property is situated." Article 145: "The parties to a contract involving foreign elements may choose the law applicable to the settlement of their contractual disputes, except as otherwise stipulated by law. If the parties to a contract involving foreign elements have not made a choice, the law of the country with which the contract has the closest connection shall be applied." Article 146: "Compensation for damages caused by a tortious act shall be governed by the *lex loci delicti*. If both parties possess the same nationality or if they are domiciled in the same country, the national law or the law of domicile of the parties may also be applicable. An act committed beyond the territory of the PRC shall not be treated as a tortious act if the law of the PRC does not deem it a tortious act." Article 147: "The marriage of a citizen of the PRC to a foreigner shall be governed by the *lex loci celebrationis*, while a divorce shall be governed by the *lex fori*." Article 148: "Maintenance shall be governed by the law of the country with which the person to be maintained has the closest connection." Article 149: "Intestate succession to a movable property shall be governed by the law of the decedent's last domicile, and intestate succession to an immovable property shall be governed by the law of the place where the immovable property is situated."

**The Rules for Implementation of the Law on Foreign-Capital Enterprises of the PRC 12 December 1990 (as modified on 12 April 2001),** Article 18: "The form of organization of a foreign-funded enterprise shall be a limited liability company. Other liability forms may be adopted upon approval. In the case of a limited liability company, the foreign investor's liability shall be limited to the amount he has contributed to the enterprise's capital. In case of any other liability form, the foreign investor shall be liable for the enterprise according to Chinese statutes and regulations." Article 48: "Any foreign-funded enterprise shall pay taxes in accordance with Chinese statutes and regulations." Article 49: "Workers and staff members of a foreign-funded enterprise shall pay individual income tax in accordance with Chinese statutes and regulations." Article 52: "Foreign exchange affairs of a foreign-funded enterprise shall be handled in accordance with Chinese regulations concerning foreign exchange control." Article 56: "A foreign-funded enterprise shall, in accordance with Chinese statutes and regulations and provisions of the financial authority, set up its own financial and accounting systems and submit them to the local financial and tax authorities for record." Article 64: "(1) A foreign-funded enterprise employing workers and staff members from China shall conclude labor contracts with the workers and staff members employed in accordance with Chinese statutes and regulations. The contract shall contain such matters as employment, dismissal, remuneration, welfare, labor protection and labor insurance. (2) No foreign-funded enterprise may employ child laborers." Article 81: "All contracts concluded between a foreign-funded enterprise and another company, enterprise or economic organization, and between a foreign-funded enterprise and any individual shall be governed by the Contract Law of the PRC."

**The Law on Adoption of the PRC of 29 February 1991 (as modified on 4 November 1998)**, Article 21: "A foreigner may, in accordance with this Law, adopt a child in the PRC. Where a foreigner wishes to adopt a child in the PRC, the matter shall be subject to examination and approval of the competent authorities of the adopter's resident country in accordance with the law of that country…"

**The Maritime Code of the PRC of 7 November 1992**, Article 268: "(1) If any international treaty concluded or acceded to by the PRC contains provisions differing from those contained in this Code, the provisions of the relevant international treaty shall be applied, unless the provisions are those on which the PRC has announced reservations. (2) International usages may be applied to matters for which neither the relevant statutes of the PRC nor international treaties concluded or acceded to by the PRC contain any relevant provisions." Article 269: "The parties to a contract may choose the law applicable to the contract, except as otherwise stipulated by law. Where the parties to a contract have made no choice, the law of the country with which the contract has the closest connection shall be applied." Article 270: "Acquisition, transfer and lapse of the ownership of a ship shall be governed by the law of the flag state of the ship." Article 271: "(1) The mortgage of a ship shall be governed by the law of the flag state of the ship. (2) If the mortgage of a ship is established before or during its bareboat charter period, the mortgage of the ship shall be governed by the law of the original country of registry of the ship." Article 272: "Maritime liens shall be governed by the *lex fori*." Article 273: "(1) Compensation for damages arising from collision of ships shall be governed by the *lex loci delicti.* (2) Compensation for damages arising from collision of ships on the high seas shall be governed by the *lex fori.* (3) Compensation for damages among colliding ships of the same nationality shall be governed by the law of the flag state, regardless of the place where the collision occurs." Article 274: "The adjustment of general average shall be governed by the law where the adjustment of general average is made." Article 275: "Restrictions of maritime compensation liabilities shall be governed by the *lex fori.*"

**The Law on Negotiable Instruments of the PRC of 5 October 1995 (as modified on 28 August 2004)**, Article 94: "(1) The application of laws to negotiable instruments involving foreign elements shall be determined in accordance with the provisions of this Chapter. (2) The term 'negotiable instruments involving foreign elements' used in the preceding paragraph refers to instruments whose issue, endorsement, acceptance, surety or payment occur both within and outside the territory of the PRC." Article 95: "(1) If any international treaty concluded or acceded to by the PRC contains provisions differing from those contained in this Law, the provisions of the relevant international treaty shall be applied, unless the provisions are those on which the PRC has announced reservations. (2) International usages may be applied to matters for which neither the relevant statutes of the PRC nor international treaties concluded or acceded to by the PRC contain any relevant provisions." Article 96: "(1) Capacity to engage in civil transactions of a debtor of negotiable instruments shall be governed by his *lex patriae.* (2) If a debtor of negotiable instruments is incapable or restrictively capable of a civil transaction in accordance with his *lex patriae*, but fully capable in accordance with the *lex loci actus*, his capacity to engage in civil transactions shall be governed by the *lex loci actus*." Article 97: "(1) Items required to be specified on bills of exchange and promissory notes at the time of issue shall be governed by the law of the place of issue. (2) Items required to be specified on cheques at the time of issue shall be governed by the law of the place of issue, but the law of the place of payment may also be applied if the parties so agree." Article 98: "Acts of endorsement, acceptance, payment and surety for negotiable instruments shall be governed by the *lex loci actus*." Article 99: "The time limit for exercising the right of recourse concerning negotiable instruments shall be governed by the law of the place of issue." Article 100: "The time limit for presenting negotiable instruments, the way of the relevant proof of refusal and the time limit for producing the proof of refusal shall be governed by the law of the place of payment." Article 101: "In case of losing negotiable instruments, the procedure of requesting preservation of negotiable instruments rights by a holder who has lost negotiable instruments shall be governed by the law of the place of payment."

**The Law on Civil Aviation of the PRC of 30 October 1995 (as modified on 27 August 2009)**, Article 185: "Acquisition, transfer and lapse of the ownership of a civil aircraft shall be governed by the law of the country of registration of the civil aircraft." Article 186: "The mortgage of a civil aircraft shall be governed by the law of the country of registration of the civil aircraft." Article 187: "The priority of a civil aircraft concerned shall be governed by the *lex fori*." Article 188: "The parties to a civil air transport contract may choose the law applicable to the contract, except as otherwise stipulated by law; where the parties to a contract have made no choice, the law of the country with which the contract has the closest connection shall be applied." Article 189: "(1) Compensation for damages to third parties on the ground caused by a civil aircraft shall be governed by the *lex loci delicti.* (2) Compensation for damages to third parties on the water surface caused by a civil aircraft in the sky over the high seas shall be governed by the *lex fori.*"

**The Contract Law of the PRC of 15 March 1999**, Article 126: "(1) The parties to a contract involving foreign elements may choose the law applicable to the settlement of their contractual disputes, except as otherwise provided by law. If the parties to a contract involving foreign elements have not made a choice, the contract shall be governed by the law of the country with which the contract has the closest connection. (2) A contract for Chinese-foreign equity joint ventures, a contract for Chinese-foreign contractual joint ventures or a contract for Chinese-foreign cooperative exploration and development of natural resources, which is to be performed within the territory of the PRC, shall be governed by the law of the PRC."

**Measures on the Registration of Adoption of Children by Foreigners in the PRC issued by the Ministry of Civil Affairs on 25 May 1999,** Article 2: "If foreigners intend to adopt children within the territory of the PRC (hereinafter referred to as 'adoption of children by foreigners in China'), they shall undertake registration in accordance with the present Measures. If a couple, one of whom is a foreigner, intends to adopt children in China, they shall also undertake registration in accordance with the present Measures." Article 3: "Foreigners intending to adopt children in China shall conform to the provisions of the relevant laws on adoption both in China and in their home countries; problems arising from the differences between the provisions of the law of their home countries and those of the Chinese law shall be resolved through consultation by relevant departments of the governments of the two countries."

**The Company Law of the PRC as modified and adopted on 27 October 2005**, Article 218: "Limited liability companies and joint stock limited companies invested by foreign investors shall be governed by this Law. Where there are different provisions in any statute regarding foreign investment, such provisions shall prevail."

# Addendum 2 Statute on the Application of Laws to Civil Relationships Involving Foreign Elements of the People's Republic of China

(Adopted by the 17th Session of the Standing Committee of the Eleventh NPC on 28 October 2010)

**Translated by CHEN Weizuo and Kevin M. Moore***

Contents



---

* CHEN Weizuo, Director of the Research Centre for Private International Law and Comparative Law, Tsinghua University School of Law, Beijing, China; Doctor of Laws, Wuhan University, China; LL.M. and *doctor iuris*, *Universität des Saarlandes*, Germany; *professeur invité à la Faculté internationale de droit comparé de Strasbourg*, France (since 2003); *professeur invité à l'Université de Strasbourg*, France (2005-2010); to be teaching the special course in French *"La nouvelle codification du droit international privé chinois"* at the Hague Academy of International Law from 30 July to 3 August 2012 during its 2012 summer session of private international law. Kevin M. Moore, LL.M., Peking University; Legislative Aide, Oregon Senator Floyd Prozanski; *juris doctor* candidate, Willamette University College of Law. The translation of this Statute is to be published in *Yearbook of Private International Law*, Vol. XII (2010), sellier. european law publishers, 2011.

## Chapter I General Provisions

Article 1 The present Statute is enacted in order to clarify the application of laws to civil relationships involving foreign elements, to solve civil disputes involving foreign elements in an equitable manner, and to safeguard the lawful rights and interests of parties.

Article 2 The law applicable to civil relationships involving foreign elements shall be determined in accordance with the present Statute. If other statutes contain special provisions on the application of laws to civil relationships involving foreign elements, those provisions shall prevail.

If the present Statute or other statutes contain no provisions with regard to the application of laws to civil relationships involving foreign elements, the law that has the closest connection with the civil relationship involving foreign elements shall be applied.

Article 3 In accordance with statutory provisions, the parties may expressly choose the law applicable to a civil relationship involving foreign elements.

Article 4 If the law of the People's Republic of China contains mandatory rules on civil relationships involving foreign elements, those mandatory rules shall be applied directly.

Article 5 If the application of a foreign law would cause harm to social and public interests of the People's Republic of China, the law of the People's Republic of China shall be applied.

Article 6 If a civil relationship involving foreign elements is to be governed by foreign law, and if different regions in the foreign country have different laws in force, the law of the region with which the civil relationship involving foreign elements has the closest connection shall be applied.

Article 7 Limitation of actions shall be governed by the law that is to govern the relevant civil relationship involving foreign elements.

Article 8 The characterization of any civil relationship involving foreign elements shall be governed by the *lex fori*.

Article 9 The law of a foreign country that is to govern a civil relationship involving foreign elements does not refer to the law on the application of laws of that country.

Article 10 The law of a foreign country that is to govern a civil relationship involving foreign elements shall be ascertained by the people's courts, arbitration institutions or administrative organs. If the parties have chosen the law of a foreign country as applicable, they shall provide the law of that country.

If the law of a foreign country cannot be ascertained, or if the law of that country contains no relevant provisions, the law of the People's Republic of China shall be applied.

## Chapter II Civil Subjects

Article 11 The civil legal capacity of a natural person shall be governed by the law of the place of his/her habitual residence.

Article 12 The capacity to engage in civil juristic acts of a natural person shall be governed by the law of the place of his/her habitual residence.

If a natural person is engaged in civil activities, and he/she has no capacity to engage in civil juristic acts according to the law of the place of his/her habitual residence, but he/she has the capacity to engage in civil juristic acts according to the *lex loci actus*, the *lex loci actus* shall be applied, except if marriage, family or succession is involved.

Article 13 Declaration of a missing person or declaration of death shall be governed by the law of the place of habitual residence of the natural person concerned.

Article 14 Matters such as the civil legal capacity, the capacity to engage in civil juristic acts, organizations and institutions of a legal person and its branches, as well as shareholders' rights and duties, shall be governed by the law of the place of registration.

If the principal place of business of a legal person differs from the place of registration, the law of the principal place of business may be applied. The place of habitual residence of a legal person is its principal place of business.

Article 15 Contents of rights of personality shall be governed by the law of the place of habitual residence of the legitimate claimant.

Article 16 Agency shall be governed by the *lex loci actus* of the act of agency, but civil relationships between the principal and the agent shall be governed by the law of the place where the agency relationship occurs.

The parties may choose by agreement the law applicable to an entrusted agency.

Article 17 The parties may choose by agreement the law applicable to a trust. In the absence of a choice by the parties, the law of the place where the trust property is situated or the law of the place where the trust relationship occurs shall be applied.

Article 18 The parties may choose by agreement the law applicable to an arbitration agreement. In the absence of a choice by the parties, the law of the place where the arbitration institution is situated or the law of the place of arbitration shall be applied.

Article 19 If the law of the country of nationality is to be applied according to the present Statute, and a natural person has two or more nationalities, the law of the country of nationality in which he/she has a habitual residence shall be applied; if he/she has no habitual residence in any country of nationality, the law of the country of nationality with which he/she has the closest connection shall be applied. If a natural person has no nationality, or if his/her nationality is unknown, the law of the place of his/her habitual residence shall be applied.

Article 20 If the law of the place of habitual residence is to be applied according to the present Statute, and the place of habitual residence of a natural person is unknown, the law of the place of his/her actual residence shall be applied.

## Chapter III Marriage and Family

Article 21 Conditions of marriage are governed by the law of the place of common habitual residence of the parties; they are governed by the law of the country of the common nationality in the absence of a place of common habitual residence; they are governed by the *lex loci celebrationis* if there exists no common nationality and the marriage is to be entered into at the place of habitual residence of one party or in his/her country of nationality.

Article 22 Formalities of marriage are valid if they satisfy the *lex loci celebrationis*, the law of the place of habitual residence or the law of the country of nationality of one party.

Article 23 Personal relationships of spouses shall be governed by the law of the place of their common habitual residence; in the absence of a place of common habitual residence, the law of the country of their common nationality shall be applied.

Article 24 With regard to property relationships of spouses, the parties may choose by agreement the law of the place of habitual residence or the law of the country of nationality of one party, or the law of the place where the principal property is situated, as applicable. In the absence of a choice by the parties, the law of the place of their common habitual residence shall be applied; in the absence of a place of common habitual residence, the law of the country of their common nationality shall be applied.

Article 25 Personal relationships and property relationships between parent and child shall be governed by the law of the place of their common habitual residence; in the absence of a place of common habitual residence, the law of the place of habitual residence or the law of the country of nationality of one party shall be applied, provided that it is the law favoring protection of the rights and interests of the weaker party.

Article 26 With regard to divorce by agreement, the parties may choose by agreement the law of the place of habitual residence or the law of the country of nationality of one party as applicable. In the absence of a choice by the parties, the law of the place of their common habitual residence shall be applied; in the absence of a place of common habitual residence, the law of the country of their common nationality shall be applied; in the absence of a common nationality, the law of the place where the institution conducting the divorce formalities is situated shall be applied.

Article 27 Divorce by litigation shall be governed by the *lex fori*.

Article 28 Conditions and formalities of adoption shall be governed by the law of the place of habitual residence of the adopter and the law of the place of habitual residence of the adoptee. Effects of adoption shall be governed by the law of the place of habitual residence of the adopter at the time of adoption. Dissolution of an adoption relationship shall be governed by the law of the place of habitual residence of the adoptee at the time of adoption or the *lex fori*.

Article 29 Maintenance shall be governed by the law of the place of habitual residence or the law of the country of nationality of one party, or the law of the place where the principal property is situated, provided that it is the law favoring protection of the rights and interests of the person to be maintained.

Article 30 Guardianship shall be governed by the law of the place of habitual residence or the law of the country of nationality of one party, provided that it is the law favoring protection of the rights and interests of the ward.

## Chapter IV Succession

Article 31 Intestate succession shall be governed by the law of the place of habitual residence of the decedent upon his/her death, but intestate succession of immovable property shall be governed by the law of the place where the immovable property is situated.

Article 32 A testament is valid as to form if the form of the testament satisfies the law of the place of habitual residence, the law of the country of nationality of the testator or the *lex loci actus* of the act of testament at the time of making the testament, or upon the death of the testator.

Article 33 The effects of a testament shall be governed by the law of the place of habitual residence or the law of the country of nationality of the testator at the time of making the testament, or upon the death of the testator.

Article 34 Matters such as the administration of estates shall be governed by the law of the place where the estates are situated.

Article 35 Devolution of estates without a successor shall be governed by the law of the place where the estates are situated upon the death of the decedent.

## Chapter V Rights *in Rem*

Article 36 Rights *in rem* of immovable property shall be governed by the law of the place where the immovable property is situated.

Article 37 The parties may choose by agreement the law applicable to rights *in rem* of movable property. In the absence of a choice by the parties, the law of the place where the movable property is situated at the time of the occurrence of the juristic fact concerned shall be applied.

Article 38 The parties may choose by agreement the law applicable to rights *in rem* of movable property that change during transport. In the absence of a choice by the parties, the law of the transport destination shall be applied.

Article 39 Securities are governed by the law of the

place where the rights of the securities are realized or other laws that have the closest connection with the securities.

Article 40 Pledge of rights shall be governed by the law of the place where the pledge is established.

## Chapter VI Creditors' Rights

Article 41 The parties may choose by agreement the law applicable to a contract. In the absence of a choice by the parties, the contract shall be governed by the law of the place of habitual residence of one party whose performance of obligations can best embody the characteristics of the contract, or by other laws that have the closest connection with the contract.

Article 42 Consumer contracts shall be governed by the law of the place of the consumer's habitual residence; if the consumer has chosen the law of the place of the provision of commodities or services as applicable, or if the entrepreneur has not been engaged in relevant business activities at the place of the consumer's habitual residence, the law of the place of the provision of commodities or services shall be applied.

Article 43 Labor contracts shall be governed by the law of the place where the laborer works; if the place where laborer works is difficult to ascertain, the law of the principal place of business of the employing unit shall be applied. Labor dispatch may be governed by the law of the dispatching place.

Article 44 Tortious liability shall be governed by the *lex loci delicti*, but it shall be governed by the law of the place of common habitual residence if the parties have a place of common habitual residence. If the parties agree to choose the applicable law after the occurrence of a tortious act, their agreement shall be followed.

Article 45 Product liability shall be governed by the law of the place of habitual residence of the person whose right has been infringed upon; if the person whose right has been infringed upon has chosen the law of the principal place of business of the infringing person or the *lex loci damni* as applicable, or if the infringing person has not been engaged in relevant business activities at the place of habitual residence of the person whose right has been infringed upon, the law of the principal place of business of the infringing person or the *lex loci damni* shall be applied.

Article 46 If rights of personality, such as right of name, right of portrait, right of reputation, or right of privacy, have been infringed upon via the internet or by any other means, the law of the place of habitual residence of the person whose right has been infringed upon shall be applied.

Article 47 Unjust enrichment or *negotiorum gestio* shall be governed by the law chosen as applicable by the parties by agreement. In the absence of a choice by the parties, the law of the place of common habitual residence of the parties shall be applied; in the absence of a place of common habitual residence, the law of the place of occurrence of the unjust enrichment or *negotiorum gestio* shall be applied.

## Chapter VII Intellectual Property Rights

Article 48 Devolution and contents of intellectual property rights shall be governed by the law of the place for which the protection is invoked.

Article 49 The parties may choose by agreement the law applicable to the transfer and licensed use of intellectual property rights. In the absence of a choice by the parties, the provisions of the present Statute relating to contracts shall be applied.

Article 50 Tortious liability arising out of infringement of intellectual property rights shall be governed by the law of the place for which the protection is invoked; after occurrence of the tortious act, the parties may also choose by agreement the *lex fori* as applicable.

## Chapter VIII Supplementary Provisions

Article 51 Where Articles 146 and 147 of the General Principles of Civil Law of the People's Republic of China, and Article 36 of the Succession Law of the People's Republic of China, differ from the provisions of the present Statute, the present Statute shall be applied.

Article 52 The present Statute shall come into force on 1 April 2011.

# Index

## Chinese Law Series

Understanding China's Criminal Procedure
YI Yanyou

**Chinese Civil Procedure and the Conflict of Laws**
CHEN Weizuo

www.ingramcontent.com/pod-product-compliance
Lightning Source LLC
LaVergne TN
LVHW091531200926
848483LV00002B/364